S0-AGT-505

Dr. & Mrs. Quentin Kintner
1105 E. Lauridsen Blvd.
Port Angeles, WA 98362

Margaret Kintner

Dr. and Mrs. Quentin Kintner
1105 E. Lauridsen Blvd.
Port Angeles, WA 98362-6639

IN THE FOOTSTEPS OF St PAUL

IN THE FOOTSTEPS OF St PAUL

WOLFGANG E. PAX

STEIMATZKY'S AGENCY
Jerusalem, Tel-Aviv, Haifa
together with
NATEEV PUBLISHING

Photographer   Elliott Faye

General Editor   Mordecai Raanan

Captions and Editing   Judith Lelyveld

Copyright © 1977
by NATEEV-Printing & Publishing Enterprises Ltd.
P. O. Box 6048, Tel-Aviv, Israel.

First printing in 1977.

Published simultaneously
in Israel by Steimatzky's Agency Ltd., Tel-Aviv
in Switzerland by Walter Verlag AG, Olten und Freiburg im Breisgau
in the Netherlands by Amsterdam Boek bv. Amsterdam.
in France by Edition Arthaud, Paris et Grenoble

ACKNOWLEDGMENTS and thanks are due to the following institutions and persons for having kindly permitted their exhibits to be photographed, and to the photographers who supplied the additional pictures: David Harris, Jerusalem, pages 13, 30, 34, 37, 40, 44, 47, 51, 58, 134, 164, 165, 170, 175, 188; Zvi Kahana, Holon, pages 14, 26, 81, 103, 131, 160, 176, 177, 182, 195, 208, 211, 215, 218, 219; Yael Braun, Jerusalem, pages 15, 16, 33, 35, 184, 189; The National Museum Villa Giulia, Rome, page 29; Israel Museum, Jerusalem, pages 30, 134; Sally Cooney, New York, page 28; Gabrielle Pax, Erlingen, F.D.R., pages 52, 53, 54, 55, 56, 57, 59, 79, 125, 128, 193, 207; Ron Ilan, Tel-Aviv, page 73; Museum of Ancient Art, Haifa, page 190; The National Maritime Museum, Haifa, page 192, end-paper.

Printed in Israel by Peli Printing Works Ltd.

CONTENTS

"I am a Jew from Tarsus." Thus his own proud assertion introduces to us one of the greatest figures in world history, the man who changed the course of Western civilization.

Saul, later known as Paul, has brought the Gospel of Christ from its cradle, the land of Israel, to the then entire known world—Asia Minor, Greece, Italy and perhaps also to the "Pillars of Hercules" at the Straits of Gibraltar. We rarely stop to consider how such an overwhelming task could have been accomplished by a single individual, with the very limited means of communication of the ancient world at his disposal. We take it for granted and as a matter of course, that the Word went forth from Jerusalem to the nations of the world. Yet it was a feat unequaled in its scope, accomplished by a man fired and driven by an idea and faith, with unique single-mindedness of purpose.

Though the story of Paul's life has been told and retold often enough, new aspects of this charismatic and elusive personality emerge, which may allow us perhaps to come closer and lift the veil, however slightly, covering the man from our inquiring gaze. It is Paul the man, not the theologian, who should be the focus of our attention when we retrace his footsteps.

The sources are far richer for Paul than for Jesus, from whom not one written word has come down to us. Thirteen letters in Paul's name, in Greek have been preserved. Of these, five are not generally considered authentic, since they only aim to support with his authority changed relationships. The definitely genuine letters were written in the short span between 51 and 58 AD and addressed to Christian communities for a specific purpose.

A further important source is the Acts of the Apostles, which according to tradition was supposed to have been written by the evangelist Luke at the end of the 1st century, that is about 40 years after Paul's letters. Acts is not a historical biography and does not seem to take cognizance of the letters. It presents a magnificent theological conception, in which the path of the Church from Jerusalem into the world is described as is pragmatically stated in the introduction: "You shall be my witness in Jerusalem and in all Judea and Samaria and to the end of the earth" (Acts 1:8). Paul is seen through the eyes of others and in the perspective of later developments as the great missionary to the nations. Therefore the conflicts which Paul had to face in his communities recede into the background, since they lost their relevance by then; the speeches are greatly emphasized, yet these are not verbatim recordings but were formulated by the writer, to present Paul as an ideal. Acts contains rich historical material, especially in the incidental remarks, but in cases of discrepancy with the Letters, the latter take precedence; sometimes archaeology, sociology and the psychology of religion can be of valuable service.

W. E. PAX

7

Thou, that stupendous truth believed,
And now the matchless deed's achieved,
Determined, dared and done,

(Christopher Smart)

1. SAUL

Rome and Paul—these names are inseparably linked and characterize the external life of Paul. Since the second century BC the Roman Empire expanded rapidly, and with the establishment of the province of Asia, covering roughly the territory of today's Turkey, the Romans were firmly entrenched in the East. Cilicia, with its capital Tarsus—Paul's birthplace— was part of the Roman world since that period, but effective Roman rule began only after Pompey's piratical drive through the East. Incidently, Cicero, the famous Roman lawyer and orator, was one of Cilicia's governors.

In the year 63 BC Pompey's legions stormed the sanctuary of Jerusalem, and Pompey himself made his assuredly ill-advised entry into its Holy of Holies. Although he did not touch any religious objects there, the outrage was unforgivable. Judaea became a protectorate. It was an established Roman policy to leave the internal administration in the hands of local rulers and to grant the local populations, especially the Jews, certain privileges. Antipater and his son Herod the Great maintained excellent relations with Rome, on whose protection they depended heavily. During Herod's lifetime and his reign of 33 years (37–4 BC) Judaea enjoyed prosperity and peace, though the king was cruel and ruthless at times. Regarded as a collaborator and usurper, Herod was thoroughly hated by the local population, and thus, in order to provide for his security in case of an uprising, he had the fortresses of Masada, Herodion and Kypros built, as well as the Antonia barracks and the citadel in Jerusalem. As a national Hellenistic ruler, on the other hand, he was deeply committed to the beauty of his capital, and had the temple restored with immense splendor and enlarged into an enclosure of about 35 acres.

Josephus Flavius compared it to "a snowy mountain glittering in the sun." The rabbinical sages, no lovers of Herod at any time, said that "whoever has not seen the House (Temple) of Herod, has not seen a beautiful edifice in his life." Pliny the elder called Jerusalem "the most splendid city not only of Judaea, but of the whole Levant."

After the death of Herod and the banishment of his son Archelaus, Judaea became a third-rank province ruled by a Roman procurator who resided in Caesarea, the harbor city founded by Herod. Jeru-

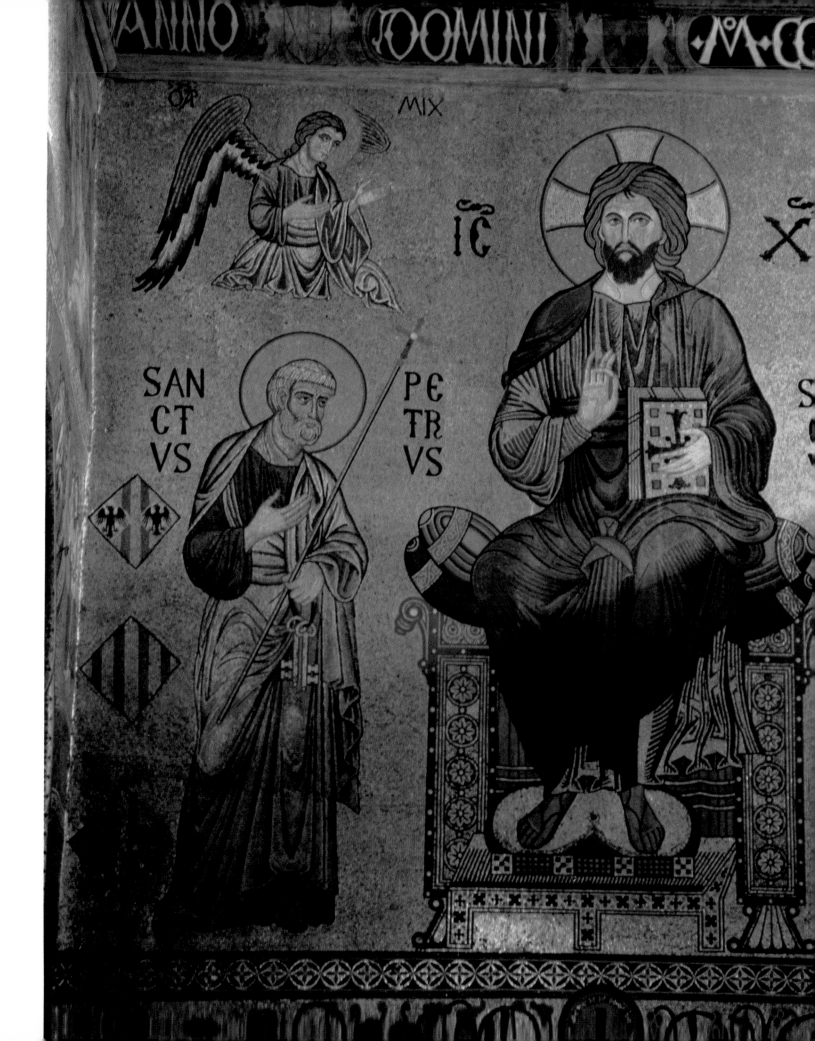

ANNO DOMINI M CC

MIX

IC XC

SANCTVS PETRVS S

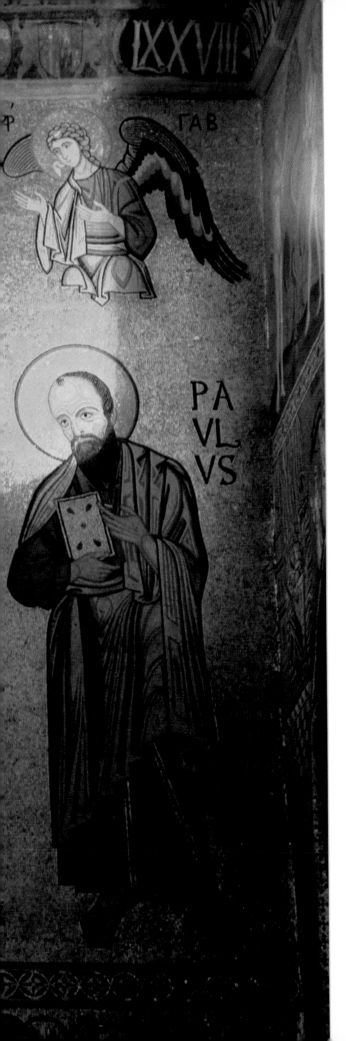

. . . Saul, who is also called Paul, filled with the Holy Spirit . . . (Acts 13:9)

Mosaic in the Chapel Palatino
at Palermo shows Christ flanked
by the apostles Paul and Peter.

salem was governed by the High Priest and the Sanhedrin and the procurators only visited the city at the times of the pilgrimage festivals. It was then that the Jews suffered most from the arrogance of the Roman legionnaires, a humiliation added to the constant yoke of repression under the Roman occupation.

Since the loss of Jewish national independence—however limited it had been—Jerusalem was no longer the capital of Judaea but became the spiritual center of Judaism. The Temple, the Sanhedrin and the famous schools of learning attracted the Diaspora Jews who sought fulfillment of their spiritual needs there. Judaism, a religion of pluralistic nature, was split into many different groups. On the political plane the Herodian party was seeking a compromise with the Romans, while the Zealots violently resented the foreign intruder, and found themselves later fighting for freedom till the bitter end. In the religious sphere the Sadducees, the high-priestly and privileged class, were at odds with the Pharisees, who stemmed mainly from the lower middle class, and whose basic teachings were concerned with the strict adherence to the written and

11

The Western Wall, known in the Christian world as the Wailing Wall, is the only vestige of the Temple Paul knew so well.

A bronze *menorah* in front of the Knesset
in Jerusalem: the top panel of the left branch
shows Hillel, the great teacher of the Law
(1st century A.D.), telling a convert who
asked to be taught the whole Torah "on one
foot" the entire essence of Jewish ethic:
"Do not do to your fellow human being what
is hateful to you". One of Hillel's disciples
was Gamaliel, who was in turn Paul's teacher.

oral law. The rise of normative Judaism at this
period is especially significant. The Samaritans were
regarded by the Jews as schismatics rather than
Gentiles, the main point of contention being the
existence of their temple on Mount Gerizim.

In addition, messianic movements were constantly
on the rise and spreading all over the country. The
sect of Qumran, a specific branch of the Essenes
living in the desert by the Dead Sea, rejected the
concept and supremacy of the Temple and its priesthood, and was awaiting the coming of the Messiah.
John the Baptist preached the baptism of repentance,
while the followers of Jesus of Nazareth, crucified
by the procurator Pontius Pilate (30 AD), maintained that their master was no other than the
Messiah, who had proclaimed that Jews as well as
non-Jews could enter the Kingdom of God.

In contrast to the Qumran sect which was living
in seclusion, Peter and the apostles were preaching
the Gospel in public in the middle of Jerusalem.
This aroused the opposition of the High Priest and
the Sadducees, who had Peter and the others arrested and arraigned before the Sanhedrin. The
majority of the Sanhedrin was for a death sentence,

I am . . . brought up . . . at the feet of Gamaliel . . . *(Acts 22:3)*

In the catacombs of Beit Shearim the tomb
of rabbi Gamaliel III, direct descendant
of Paul's teacher, carries the inscription
(left) reading in Hebrew: "This (tomb) is
of rabbi Gamaliel". Celebrating the *seder*
feast (right) on the first night of Passover,
the festival of the Exodus. Steeped deeply
in the Jewish tradition, Paul adhered strictly
to the celebration of festivals.

but Gamaliel, the grandson of the famous Hillel, and himself an acknowledged authority on the Law, opposed it: "Keep away from these men and let them alone. For if this plan or this undertaking is of men, it will fail; but if it is of God, you will not be able to overthrow them. You might even be found opposing God" (Acts 5:58). What was then, the reaction of Saul, one of Gamaliel's students?

THE JEW

In the Temple of Jerusalem, Paul once gave details about his person, which appear to be authentic: "I am a Jew from Tarsus in Cilicia, a citizen of no mean city, but brought up in this city at the feet of Gamaliel" (Acts 21:39; 22:3). He stressed time and again his Jewish descent, with its religious significance, besides the national one, when answering his opponents: "Circumcized on the eighth day, of the people of Israel, of the tribe of Benjamin, a Hebrew born of Hebrews" (Phil. 3:5). He expressly emphasized his connection with the tribe of Benjamin which gave Israel its first king, Saul, the namesake of Paul. Moreover, Benjamin enjoyed a particular position of honor, as the only one of

. . . and you shall teach them diligently to your children . . .

(Deuteronomy 6:7)

In the *heder*, the primary school for orthodox Jewish children,
loud repetition of the sacred texts of the Bible is a hallowed
tradition. The boys memorize the text which, indeed,
they retain throughout their lives.

Jacob's sons born in the Holy Land and therefore the "Shekhina", the glory of God, was with him. The fact that Paul stressed his descent all through his life shows how deeply rooted he was in the oriental-patriarchal world which stood in sharp contrast to the Hellenistic world stamped strongly with individualism.

What did Paul look like? Though countless representations of his person were made through the ages by artists the world over, there is none by his contemporaries. The little we know comes from a 2nd century legend telling how Paul was recognized by a man who had never seen him before, through this description: a man of short stature, bow-legged, bald-headed with bushy eyebrows grown together over a prominent nose, of noble carriage and good-natured countenance, a man indistinguishable from countless thousands who, from times immemorial, have walked the shores of the Mediterranean basin. It is only in his speech that the extraordinary effect he had on people came to the fore. The fascination he exerted on his listeners was at times so great, that he was on occasion called "a trickster".

In order to understand Paul better, one has to take a closer look at his Jewish heritage, which was an integral part of his personality. Saul grew up as a member of a conservative Pharisaic family, which by virtue of its Hebrew descent certainly knew Hebrew and Aramaic. One of the pages of glory in the history of Judaism is the development, since earliest times, of high quality education of children in the family and in the community. Family prayer on the Sabbath and on other holidays played a key role in this. Knowledge of the Torah and the Commandments, as well as the history of the Passover tradition, afforded a special opportunity for it. In the book of Deuteronomy 6:20–25, the father is expressly enjoined to instruct his son: "When your son asks you in time to come, 'What is the meaning of the testimonies and the statutes and the ordinances which the Lord our God has commanded you?' then you shall say to your son, 'We were Pharaoh's slaves in Egypt; and the Lord brought us out of Egypt with a mighty hand . . . that he might bring us in and give us the land which he swore to our fathers. And the Lord commands us to do all these statutes, to fear the Lord our God, for our good always, that he might preserve us alive as at this day'."

According to tradition Paul's family came
from Gush Halav (Giscala) in Galilee. A
prosperous Jewish town in ancient times,
noted for its fine silks and oil, it is today the
center of Maronite Christians.

The primary school was in the vicinity of the synagogue. Children began their education early, at the age of four. In the Testament of Levi, parents were admonished: "Teach your children Scripture, so that they have understanding throughout their entire life by continually reading the law of God" (13:2). The alphabet was learned on wax tablets. As for the Greeks Homer was the central text, so for the Jews it was the Torah, which one began to study with the book of Genesis. For the beginners the teaching method was loud repetition of the master's words; later the students had to read aloud, as the famous rabbi Samuel had admonished: "Open your mouth and read the Scriptures, open your mouth and learn the Talmud, that your studies may be retained . . ." (Erubin, 54 a). Just how much the school preserved the Jewish heritage and how great was its importance in preserving their nationality was acknowledged by the philosopher of the Cynic school, Oinomaos of Gadara, one of the cities of the Decapolis, on the eastern bank of the Jordan: "Go and observe their synagogues and houses of study; as long as you find these children chirping away—reciting the Torah aloud—you cannot make

any impression on them. For their heavenly Father is standing by their side."

According to tradition, Saul's family came from Giscala in the Upper Galilee, the present day Gush Halav. The locality was very prosperous, noted especially for its exports of oil and silk. The ruins of two synagogues dating from the 3rd century AD in Meron and Giscala, as well as graves of famous sages from Jerusalem from the 1st century AD, testify to the deep piety of the local population. Its spirit lives on albeit in different guises: Meron is the citadel of Jewish orthodoxy, the neighboring Gush Khalav the center of Maronite Christians.

TARSUS, "NO MEAN CITY"
Under the pressure of the Roman occupation, the parents or the grandparents of Saul moved voluntarily or under duress to Tarsus, the capital of the Roman province of Cilicia, in Asia Minor, where Saul was born about 10 AD, a son of one of the numerous Jewish emigrant families.

Tarsus was located on the Cydnus, praised by the Roman poet Tibullus: "noiselessly, deep-blue, it gently winds its way through its bed with calm waters." It was the river Cleopatra had sailed with Mark Anthony in 41 BC. Shakespeare made it immortal:

"The barge she sat it, like a burnished throne,
Burn'd on the water . . . ."

Tarsus had been founded by the Phoenicians, and despite later Hellenization, it retained its oriental character. Under Roman rule, the city had various privileges which explained the fact that Paul possessed by birth Roman imperial citizenship, in addition to the municipal one. He was proud of it, and stressed it later on several occasions. This is also the origin of his Roman name "Paul", while his family and friends called him "Saul".

The city lived primarily from sea traffic and caravan commerce. Fishing also flourished, the moray of Tarsus being considered a special delicacy. There was a prosperous textile industry, too, and Saul was apprenticed to the family business, which specialized in the manufacture of a tough goat-hair fabric, used in the making of tents.

Today Tarsus is a dusty little Turkish town, under which, scarcely excavated, the old city slumbers. The only monument to its former glory is a ruined gateway called "Paul's Arch" as well as "Cleopatra's Gate" but it is in fact of a later date.

In Tarsus we encounter the world of Hellenism, i.e. the expansion of Greek culture and civilization, a movement which began with the conquests of Alexander the Great and continued into Roman times. Characteristic of this period were the establishment and expansion of numerous cities, as described in Plutarch in his study of Alexander: "Alexander established more than seventy cities among savage tribes and sowed all Asia with Grecian magistracies and thus overcame its uncivilized and brutish manner of living. Egypt would not have its Alexandria, nor Mesopotamia its Seleucia, nor Caucasus its Greek City, for by the founding of cities in these places savagery was extinguished, and the worse element gaining familiarity with the better, changed under its influence" (328 ff.). In contrast to the rural countryside of Israel, which had only small townships, here large cities dominated: by the beginning of the Christian era their number reached 330. Temples, gymnasia, city halls, theaters and market places characterized all of them, being the hallmark of Hellenistic civilization. Yet they were not mono-

The ruins of a 3rd century synagogue in
Meiron, the neighbor and contemporary of
Gush Halav. With the destruction of the
Temple, Jewish worship abandoned sacrifice,
and prayers combined with the teaching
of the law centered in the synagogues.

tonous, exhibiting a great variety of forms, and reflecting the pride of their citizens whose ambition was to outshine the others as a cultural center. Accordingly, Tarsus had a university which competed with that of Athens.

Philosophy flourished in Tarsus, especially that of the Stoics—Augustus himself had been a pupil of a Tarsian Stoic. Athenodorus had instructed the future teacher of Augustus to write all the letters of the alphabet ere he got excited. Tarsus was a Stoic stronghold; two of the most distinguished successors of Zeno, who gave the world Stoic ideas, came from Tarsus.

In the academic-philosophical-theological discussions of the Stoics, the ideal of the human personality occupied a central position. They held an uncompromising belief in eternal order which must be also the law of our own nature. The ideal was, therefore, of self-improvement to reach perfection.

The Epicureans, on the other hand, stressed indifference towards the world and "equanimity" as their goal—to be guarded against all unpleasantness. The unifying bond for all was the Greek language which supplanted the local dialects.

Meiron contains the traditional tomb of rabbi Shimon Bar-Yohai, the reputed father of the *Cabbala*. In his honour are conducted the annual celebrations of *Lag Ba'omer* (33 days after the count of sheaths), the presumed date of his death, when thousands of orthodox Jews throng to the village with their families, dancing and singing.

22

That Saul was initially influenced by the Stoics is evident from his writings. This is of particular interest, since the founder of Stoicism, Zeno, was not a Greek, but like Saul a Semite, from Kittium on Cyprus. Saul's vernacular was Hellenistic Greek, of which he had masterly command, and to which he contributed a personal style excelled by few. He had also studied the Scriptures in the Standard Greek version, known as the Septuagint, which was made in Alexandria in the 3rd or 2nd century BC.

One of the most significant features of that period was the large number of Jews living in the Diaspora, numerically several times greater than the population of Judaea itself. They spread from the 4th century BC onwards, especially into the cities of Asia Minor. "There is no people in the world among whom part of our brethren is not found" (Josephus, Wars 2, 398). They always settled in groups, forming a nucleus of a community, and often enjoyed numerous privileges. An edict of Augustus reaffirms their rights to live "according to their ancestral customs, to send money to Jerusalem and to keep the Sabbath. Persons stealing Jewish holy books or sacred funds from synagogues are defined as sacri-

legious" (Josephus, Antiquities, 16, 162–165). But of special importance was the fact that each of them had the reassuring feeling of belonging to one family. Every visitor or new arrival would find his "co-religionists", usually in the synagogue, who would introduce him into the ways of the place, and would stand by him in time of need with advice and aid. The synagogue was of course, an obligatory feature; no community, however poor, would dispense with having one. It usually stood in the center of the quarter and was the focus of the congregation's spiritual as well as social life.

A particular characteristic of the Diaspora was the Jews' attachment to "Eretz Israel", the Land of Israel. Many fulfilled their obligation of a pilgrimage to Jerusalem and the payment of the customary "half-shekel", as well as contributed voluntary offerings in gold or silver to the Temple. A special institution were the envoys ("apostles") coming from Judaea, who supervised the administration and proclaimed the holy days.

Their severe monotheism, their holy days—especially the Sabbath with its lights—the feeling of community responsibility and a high awareness of

I am a Jew, from Tarsus in Cilicia, a citizen of no mean city

(Acts 21:39)

Tarsus on the Cydnus river was the birthplace of Paul. Among the principal remains of that ancient city is the Roman-Byzantine gate, called Cleopatra's Gate, but is actually of a much later period.

Some also of the ... Stoic philosophers met him *(Acts 17:18)*

Zeno of Kitium, Cyprus, the founder of the Stoic school. Since Tarsus was famous for its Stoic School, we may find an echo of its doctrine in Paul's teachings.

the need of bringing the religious message to the heathen, attracted many God-fearing folk. These so-called "God-fearers" observed the Sabbath and the dietary laws and paid their share of the Temple tax. But they did not take the final step of circumcision which is mandatory for a convert into the Jewish faith. It was among these "God-fearers" that Paul found his main following. And though the Jews formed part of the overall Hellenistic culture, they regarded themselves essentially as Hebrews.

What was Paul's attitude as a Jew, toward Hellenistic culture? He knew all about the sports of the city; the running, the boxing, the wrestling. This is reflected in his imagery: "Do you know that in a race all the runners compete, but only one receives the prize? So run that you may obtain it. Every athlete exercises self-control in all things. They do it to receive a perishable wreath, but we an imperishable" (I Cor. 9:24–27).

The Jews abhorred Hellenistic sports which were associated with pagan sacrifices and conducted in the nude. The establishment of a sports gymnasium in Jerusalem at the time of the high priest Jason

A citizen of a Hellenistic city, Paul was thoroughly familiar with athletics, an inseparable feature of the Greek way of life, and their influence is reflected in his imagery which he used as a precept for moral self-improvement. A boxing match (right) and a running contest (left) painted on Greek vases dating from the 6th century B.C.

was considered by the Pharisees a great sacrilege. Also the Stoic from Syria, Poseidon, saw gymnasia only as places of loafing and superfluous indulgence in luxury. Thus, by virtue of his strict Pharisaic upbringing and the later Stoic influence, Saul certainly would not have participated in any sports activities. It would be interesting to speculate on Paul's attitude toward the everyday life in his native city. Although as governor of Cilicia in 51–50 BC the famous Cicero visited Tarsus frequently, Paul, living in a Jewish milieu, would know nothing of the man and his writings.

The Hellenistic man was very much aware of his surroundings and concerned with their aesthetic aspect. The cult of external beauty was one of the features of the culture of the Hellenists. They delighted in pastoral landscapes and spacious flourishing gardens, described in numerous poems and finding expression as well in pictorial art. King Herod, though a Jew, was thoroughly Hellenized in this respect; his winter palace in Jericho, recently excavated, was complete with wide, well-watered gardens, stoas, swimming pools, decorative niches and rare potted plants. Paul shows no interest in

do not box as one beating the air

(I Corinthians 9 : 24–26)

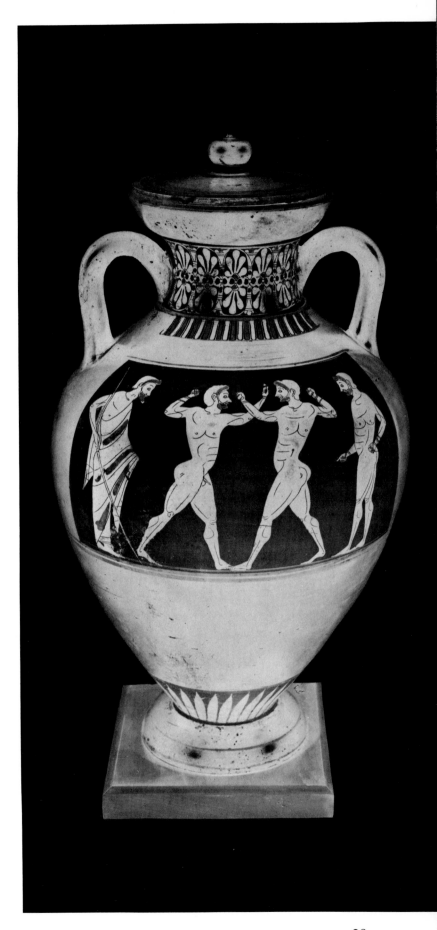

this aspect of gracious living. In this respect he was completely unaffected by Hellenism, steeped as he was in the Jewish tradition which was primarily concerned with the dynamics of an event rather than its external trappings.

The Hellenistic city had however its social problems. People streamed from the countryside into the city where they felt uprooted and isolated. The large numbers of foreign workers coming from Greece to Asia Minor, Syria and Egypt, changing masters ever so often, were typical of the period. Insecurity and uncertainty were the hallmarks of the life of the lower middle classes in the Hellenistic towns. But it was as well a period characterized by a quest for religious expression, prompted perhaps by the realization of the precariousness of human existence. The god of healing Asclepius, the goddess of fate Tyche, various mystery rites and strange superstitions, all had their followers. Oriental religions were of particular attraction, either for the novelty of the experience, or as promising salvation.

And you shall write them on the doorposts of your houses and on your gates (Deuteronomy 6:9)

The *mezuza*, a small wooden or metal capsule containing a strip of parchment with the Jewish confession of faith: "Hear, O Israel: The Lord our God is one Lord" (Deut. 6:4), has been affixed to the doorposts of all Jewish dwellings, public gates and buildings since the most ancient times as it is still today.

THE SCHOLAR

In an observation on the periods of a man's life the Talmud states that a child should begin Bible study at the age of five, the study of the Mishna at ten, fulfillment of the commandments at thirteen, the study of the Talmud at fifteen, and be married at eighteen (Abot 5, 21). The end of the twelfth year was an especially important point in the life of a young Jew, since at this point he is Bar Mitzva, "a son of the Law"; he has attained his majority from the point of view of his religion and is responsible for his acts. In Jerusalem the youth was customarily brought to the elders, so that he should be bound to the Law by them. The story of the 12-year-old Jesus having a discussion with the elders is a significant example. We do not know where and when Saul became Bar Mitzva. In any case, we find Saul at the beginning of his secondary studies in Jerusalem, where the family had close ties, since his sister and nephew lived there.

The everyday life of the young student was probably none too different from his life in Tarsus. On the right side of the entrance to his home, on the doorpost, a "mezuza" would have been affixed. This small metal or wooden capsule, containing a strip of parchment bearing the confession of faith from Deuteronomy 6:4–9: "Hear, O Israel: The Lord our God is one Lord; and you shall love the Lord your God with all your heart, and with all your soul and with all your might", is meant to remind the family constantly that it is subject to the word of God. The finding of such a "mezuza" in the caves of Qumran on the Dead Sea shows that in Paul's time, as today, it was attached to all Jewish houses and public gates and buildings.

At the time of prayer Saul would have worn the liturgical vestments, the prayer straps called "tefillin", on the forehead and left arm. These too, have been found in the Dead Sea caves, one specimen from the period before 70 AD, another from the time of Bar Kochba (about 135 AD). The figure of the pious Jew with his "tefillin" is a usual sight in Orthodox Jewish circles, one that has often been depicted by Marc Chagall in his paintings.

Saul would have covered his head and shoulders with the "tallit", the prayer shawl still customary today. And he would have observed the numerous dietary regulations, according to which the consumption of blood and flesh of certain unclean beasts (such as the pig) and certain fish was forbidden. The problem of food being "kosher" (i.e. fit for consumption) was a very current one in Paul's time, if we consider the rulings set forth at the convention of the Apostles (Acts 15:21). In general, celebration of the liturgy in the Temple and in household communions stood at the center of religious life.

Jerusalem was above all a city of schools. According to a rabbinic observation, there were 480 synagogues and each had a school building and a "beth-hamidrash" (house of study)—classes for instruction in the Bible and in the Mishna. The foundations for this had been laid by the sages who in turn stemmed from the schools of the prophets. Among the sages, Ben Sirach, ca. 180 BC, stands out. He called upon the young people: "Draw near to me, you who are untaught and lodge in my school. . . . get these things for yourselves without money. Put your neck under the yoke and let your soul receive instruction" (50:23–26). While the old scribal schools were exclusive, Ben Sirach began a development which was to encompass the entire people. A psalm

31

found in Qumran states that wisdom is given in order to proclaim the glory of God, to make his power known to the fools and to explain his greatness to those who lack understanding.

Instruction was free of charge, so that the teacher had to practice a craft. Paul too never gave up his of tentmaking. It is a noteworthy point, that the teachers were no longer anonymous, but personalities in their own right, whose sayings and anecdotes were preserved and later collected in the tractate Abot. When Saul came to Jerusalem he was therefore able to select his teachers. The choice was by no means simple, since there were various talents and trends of thought. Paul's choice fell upon the tolerant and wise Gamaliel the Elder, a grandson of the famous and saintly Hillel. By Gamaliel Saul was introduced to the history and theology of his people and became familiar with the methods of scriptural exegesis, which he applied later time and again in his letters. Questions and answers, according to firmly established principles, including even the use of fictitious opponents, were characteristic of this mode of instruction. It aimed at the overall educa-

tion of the man and not the mere imparting of knowledge. Therefore the personal relations between the teacher and pupil were very important, as the dialogue went beyond the discussion of learned questions and touched on all aspects of life. We can assume that the relationship between Gamaliel and his students involved personal attention to each of them, a distinctive achievement of the Pharisaic schools.

It is not certain whether Saul, who had had such an outstanding education, was ordained a rabbi. It is just as hard to answer the question of whether he was married. According to the Talmudic rule of conduct cited above, at the age of eighteen the young Jew was supposed to marry, an injunction all the more obligatory for a rabbi. Rabbi Eliezer explained it clearly (90 AD): "He who does not engage in propagation of the race is as though he shed blood" (Yabamoth 63 b). The fact that rabbis felt called upon to take such a strong stand on this point proves that there were reluctant bridegrooms and exceptions. These included Simeon Ben Azzai, to whom it was said: "Some preach well and act well, others act well but do not preach well; you

And these words . . . shall be as frontlets between your eyes

(Deuteronomy 6:6–8)

A Jew at prayer. Paul too would have covered
his head and shoulders with the *tallith*—
the prayer shawl, and would have worn the
teffilin—black cubic capsules containing
sheets of parchment with Biblical texts.

... *and you shall talk of them when you walk by the way ...*

(Deuteronomy 6:6–7)

Instruction in the Law was developed by the Pharisees
into a system of education due to encompass the entire
people. In Paul's time, as it is still today, the *beth
hamidrash* (house of study) and the *yeshiva* (right) became
the colleges of higher studies of the Oral Law. A father
instructing his young son on their way to
the synagogue (below).

I am a Jew, . . . educated according to the strict manner of the law of our fathers, . . . (Acts 22:3)

Then they cast him (Stephen) out of the city and stoned him

however, preach well but do not act well", to which the rabbi answered: "But what shall I do, seeing that my soul is in love with the Torah; the world can be carried on by others." Saul was a self-willed personality, quite capable of disregarding this tradition. This view is perhaps supported by the fact that at the time when he wrote the first letter to the Corinthians, he had no wife, and showed a certain restraint when speaking to his faithful about marriage (7:1–9). On the other hand he firmly asserts the fact that he had been raised according to the strict manner of the law of his ancestors. One possible deduction is that he had been married and was widowed young, perhaps already at the time of his calling.

THE YOUNG HOTHEAD
Saul had never met Jesus, for he came to Jerusalem shortly after the crucifixion. The new Nazarene movement in Jerusalem consisted of two distinct groups: the conservative, Aramaic-speaking "Hebrews" and the "Hellenists"—a more progressive minded community hailing from the Greek-speaking Diaspora Jewry. They differed in their outlook in

The southeast corner of the Temple esplanade which, according to an early tradition, was the site where St. Stephen met his death by stoning, and where later St. James was martyred too.

more than one respect; but of special importance was the fact that they were not of one mind in their position on the Law and Temple, to which the Hebrews held on tenaciously, and of which the Hellenists—in a radical continuation of Jesus' teachings—became critical opponents. Therefore they were sympathetic to the sect of the Samaritans living in Samaria who for similar reasons were separate from the Orthodox Jews. While the Hebrews, conservative as they were, kept in the background—the Hellenists, who as former Diaspora Jews had a stronger missionary motivation, moved out into public life. Hailing from the thriving cosmopolitan Hellenistic cultural world, the Hellenists also found the locals, few of whom could speak Greek, somewhat primitive. Though seemingly insignificant, often sociological rather than ideological in character, these differences were to put a poignant stamp on Saul's future labor of love.

Among the followers of the new movement was a young man called Stephen. He was chosen by the apostles to tend to the needs of the elderly and the widows of the community. He did more than the special task assigned to him; he accomplished wonders in his work and in the preaching of the gospel. But he was reproached for never ceasing "to speak words against the Holy Place and Law; for we have heard him say that this Jesus of Nazareth will destroy this place and will change the customs which Moses delivered to us" (Acts 6:13). It was obvious that the Pharisees, deeply committed to the observance of the Law and holiness of the Temple, would not countenance such an approach. So when Stephen incensed the crowd one day beyond bearing, he was charged with blasphemy and subversion of the establishment, and arraigned before the Sanhedrin. And when he made a brilliant defence, tumult arose: "They cried out with a loud voice and stopped their ears and rushed together upon him."

Then "they cast him (Stephen) out of the city and stoned him" (Acts 7:57–58). The place of the stoning was the southeast corner of the Temple wall, where the terrain slopes sharply into the Kidron valley; there later, James met his death in the same way. In the times of the Crusades, the place was determined to have been in the vicinity of the present day "Stephen's Gate".

Stephen having been successfully disposed of,

other members of his group were pursued, jailed or banished from the City. But actually only the Hellenistic circles were affected, while the apostles with their conservative adherents were able to remain in Jerusalem unmolested. It is noteworthy that it was not the messianism of Jesus which was the real ground for the persecution of his followers, since Judaism had often known groups which proclaimed one or another "prophet" the messiah; it was the negative stand on and the unrelenting criticism of the Temple and the Law which were the foremost reasons. Thus the persecutions, though not officially condemned, were also not openly declared policy but rather inspired and carried out by fanatical fringe groups, with which Saul was associated. By his own words, he was "as to zeal a persecutor of the church" (Phil. 3:6). The book of Acts gives, for understandable reasons, much too great a weight to these actions, which in reality were limited and by no means exceptional in the context of the political, social and religious ferment of the times.

Yet the New Faith, in spite of the persecutions, continued to spread, to Samaria as well as to Damascus, which was one of the "Decapolis" (the Ten Cities, or Greek colonies in the Levant), with a strong Jewish element. It had been leased by Caligula, Tiberius' successor, to King Aretas IV of the Nabateans, whose attitude, nevertheless, toward the Romans, corresponded to the one held by the Jews. Thus the relations between Jerusalem and Damascus were sufficiently close for the spreading of the New Faith to be considered a threat in Jerusalem's extreme circles. Therefore Saul must have made up his mind to try to eradicate the new "heresy" from Damascus too, where, in the meantime, it had struck a firm root. But since the authority of the Sanhedrin did not extend beyond Judaea, Saul, setting out on his journey, could not have had any official documents with him, only letters of recommendation to the leaders of the Jewish community in Damascus.

A later tradition views St. Stephen's Gate as the site
of Stephen's martyrdom. Called also the Lions' Gate,
it owes its name to the reliefs of two pairs of lions
which flank the entrance. Through this gate enters
the procession on Palm Sunday.

2. THE CALLING

The journey to Damascus was long and strenuous. Saul and his companions pressed northward. Their route would take them past Samaria's undulating brown-green terraced hills, across the black-earthed, fertile Valley of Jezre'el, down to the lusciously verdant, tropical Jordan valley, where they would cross the river. The hardest part of their journey was yet to come; the long, steep climb from the Sea of Galilee, whose shores Jesus had but recently walked happily with his disciples, and up to Damascus, more than two thousand feet above it. Finally, the beautiful city came into sight, with snow-capped Mount Hermon towering above it. And here, before the gates of Damascus, occurred that dramatic event, shattering in its poignancy, which was to give Saul's life such a fateful new turn.

THE VISION

"As he journeyed he approached Damascus, and suddenly a light from heaven flashed about him. And he fell to the ground and heard a voice saying to him, 'Saul, Saul, why do you persecute me?' And he said, 'Who are you, Lord?' And he said, 'I am Jesus, whom you are persecuting; but rise and enter

the city, and you will be told what you are to do'. The men who were traveling with him stood speechless, hearing the voice, but seeing no one. Saul arose from the ground; and when his eyes were opened, he could see nothing; so they led him by the hand and brought him into Damascus" (Acts 9:3–9).

A modern reader may take a sceptical view of such a story which, since it does not enter into the scope of ordinary human experience, defies his imagination. In consequence he is readily inclined to consider it a fable or a legend. But here we are not faced with a case of a stenographic record of an everyday event. It is a religious phenomenon far outside the range of methods of historical investigation, but nonetheless a reality of decisive influence on Paul's life.

A narration of a religious experience is like a symphony, in which a theme is sounded, picked up by other instruments and repeated in numerous variations, while the secondary voices provide the background. It can also be likened to a painting wherein the details are of no importance, but which impresses itself upon the mind of the viewer by the overall composition of color and line, and either pleases or shocks him. But a narrator of a religious revelation is compelled to present, in human verbal terms, this material which yet does not belong to the world of human experience. All these phenomena are not external events as such, but ancient Jewish religious symbols, which are but the framework to the one fact—that Paul, at the gates of Damascus, was overpowered by a force which did not come from inside him, which did not originate in the narrower or wider compass of his life, but which had its origin outside him. A personal encounter with God always takes place in the innermost part of man into which no outsider can penetrate; it can only be observed with awe. The experience though would be best served in Hamlet's words: "There are more things in heaven and earth, Horatio, than are dreamt of in your philosophy." For Saul it remained a mystery—a word which played a significant role in his theology and which he was to spend the rest of his life analyzing and expounding. All he did understand was that he was given the grace to hear and to follow his Lord.

Still in shock from his experience, he was "led by the hand" into the city, to lodge with a certain Judas, perhaps an inkeeper, in the street called Straight. It is still so called in Arabic, and is still a main artery. Saul stayed there—but let the author of Acts resume his touching tale—". . . and for three days he was without sight, and neither ate nor drank. Now there was a disciple at Damascus named Ananias. The Lord said to him in a vision, 'Ananias . . . rise and go to the street called Straight, and inquire in the house of Judas for a man of Tarsus, named Saul . . .'". Ananias was then ordered to "lay his hands on him so that he might regain his sight." Ananias objected: "I have heard from many about this man, how much evil he has done to thy saints at Jerusalem." But the Voice replied: "Go, for he is a chosen instrument of mine to carry my name before the Gentiles and kings and the sons of Israel; for I will show him how much he must suffer for the sake of my name." Ananias did as he was commanded; went to see Saul and laying his hands on him told him that he had been sent by Jesus whom Saul had encountered on his journey. "And immediately something like scales fell from his (Saul's) eyes and he regained his sight (Acts 9:3–18).

The mention of Saul's baptism does not usually

arrest our attention, since for us, baptism is so very much a matter of course. But in antiquity, people were much more conscious of the significance of immersion and bathing. For the Greeks, bathing in the waters of a spring or a river in a given place meant that the bather could settle there and acquire the rights of a citizen. For the Jews, immersion is a symbol of purity of body and soul, and mandatory for proselytes entering the Jewish faith. In his surviving writings, Paul mentioned baptism several times, but never referred to his own. It marked for him the crossing of a line from death to life, and the entering in the communion of Jesus Christ. He spoke of his experience with great reluctance, and usually only when provoked. He never spoke of Jesus' earthly life which he knew only from the mouths of others; rather were all his words overshadowed by his unique encounter with Him. It also emphasized his independence, since he had been called directly by the Lord and "by the grace of God". His calling, he would stress time and again, was "not from men nor through man, but through Jesus Christ", and the Gospel made known to him was "not man's gospel". "For I did not receive it from man, nor was

I taught it, but it came through a revelation of Jesus Christ" (Gal. 1:1, 11–12).

His thirst for spiritual fulfillment, his intellectual striving for a direct "Though and I" dialogue with his God and his need for prayer, attested to by every page of his letters, was his Jewish heritage which he had absorbed in his family and in the school of Gamaliel. Thus it was his profound religious involvement, first steeped in traditional Judaism, which contributed largely, and finally paved the way, to his ultimate conversion (32 AD).

Damascus is holy ground. Not far from the "Straight" street stands Ananias' house converted into a chapel. Outside the town, in the cemetery is a sacred rock—so often the site of revelation in the Orient—and therefore pointed out as the place where Paul had his vision. One of the minarets of the great mosque of Damascus bears the name of Jesus—as the site where he will again step upon earth on the day of Last Judgment. And to the north of the city a mountain is pointed out on which according to the Koran, Abraham had his great illumination: he saw a star, the moon and the sun rising and disappearing and said: "O my people, I

View of the beautiful fertile Jordan valley with the southern tip of the Sea of Galilee shimmering in the distance. Paul would have crossed the valley and the river on his way to Damascus.

44

am free from your idolatry. See, I turn my face to the creator of Heaven and earth" (6:75–79).

THE CONVERT

There is an old saying that at Damascus Saul became Paul. This however, does not reflect the truth, since also after his conversion Paul remained conscious of his Jewish heritage. Only in the light of Jesus does Jewish theology take on a different aspect: the Torah loses its dominant position and must be interpreted on the basis of the gospel. One can therefore understand Paul's outburst of emotion, so typical of converts, when he says: "Whatever gain I had, I counted as a loss for the sake of Christ. Indeed I count everything as a loss because of the surpassing worth of knowing Jesus Christ my Lord. For his sake I have suffered the loss of all things and count them as refuse in order that I may gain Christ" (Phil. 3:8).

For the period immediately following his calling, we have his own authentic words: "I did not confer with flesh and blood, nor did I go up to Jerusalem to those who were apostles before me, but I went into Arabia; and again returned to Damascus" (Gal. 1:17). If he did not go to Jerusalem, it was not a question of not wanting to acknowledge the other apostles' authority. True, he felt himself their equal because of the call of the Lord, but above all he did not want to waste time, since he believed the end of the world and Jesus' second coming in judgment imminent. Therefore he attached no importance whatever to the observance of the patriarchal custom according to which Peter had precedence as the head of the community. That Paul disregarded "protocol", to which all in the East are most sensitive, is abundant evidence of how charged he was with the dynamism of his mission. From this it would follow that he did not retreat into solitude, for that would be at odds with his clear and express commission to preach. A dialogue with God always means a mission; in Paul's case it meant bringing the Gospel to the world.

"Arabia" in this context, meant the kingdom of the Nabateans, ruled by King Aretas IV, whose capital was Petra. His kingdom extended from Damascus (temporarily under his rule), across Transjordan and present-day Saudi Arabia. It was the only region where an Arab population had estab-

It was from the shores of the enchanging Sea of Galilee (Lake Gennazareth) which Jesus had but recently walked, that Paul began the steep climb toward Damascus. Most of Jesus' ministry had been devoted to the serene fishermen villages in the neighborhood of the lake, where he had spent the happiest years of his life.

lished a state which was deeply influenced by Hellenism. Saul was probably familiar with the Nabateans from his days in Jerusalem, as due to their close ties with the Jews, they often came across the Jordan into Judaea. The "Wise Men from the East" were most certainly Nabateans. Just where Saul was active we do not know, but he would have worked in the region southeast of Damascus, a volcanic area with fertile fields, where the population was of a tenatiously conservative nature and has preserved its ancestral customs to this very day. In such a setting Paul could not have been very successful.

The Nabateans were originally a Beduin tribe of highwaymen, who in time developed into excellent caravan leaders, which meant they engaged in what is best described by the modern term "international commerce". Their organizational talent was unsurpassed, and they had agencies in the entire ancient world. A central point appears to have been Palmyra, where the "letters of thanks" left behind by grateful travelers are still preserved in stone. Among the Nabateans, Saul as a tentmaker would have been in great demand. Perhaps through them

he became familiar with the customary routes which these ancient "Cook & Sons" traveled. Over these routes they forwarded the rich treasures of inner Arabia from the Persian Gulf and the Red Sea through Syria and Asia Minor to Europe. Their ships under the emblem of a dolphin sailed from the Mediterranean ports of El-Arish in Sinai, Gaza, Ashkelon, Caesarea and Antioch to the great import harbor of Italy, Pozzuoli. They left their traces in every corner of the ancient civilized world. The Romans had in a large measure fitted their road network onto that of the Nabateans. Looking at a map and tracing the caravan and shipping routes of the Nabateans, one sees that with the inclusion of the port of Pozzuoli, they correspond almost exactly to the routes Saul traveled.

Having roused opposition in Arabia, he was forced to return to Damascus. There too he was met, particularly by the Jewish community, with open hostility and compelled to flee. "The governor under King Aretas guarded the city of Damascus in order to seize me, but I was let down in a basket through a window in the wall and escaped his hands" (II Cor. 11:32). In order to understand such means of escape, one must envision a house, of which the city wall formed the rear wall. Wicker or leather baskets, lowered and raised by a reel, were a common device for hauling articles. One such leather basket could until very recently be seen on the wall of the St. Catherine monastery in Sinai. Saul's escape must have taken place from such a house, for once safely on the ground, he was actually deposited outside the city walls.

For Saul, his precipitate secret flight from Damascus, the city of his enlightenment, must have come as a shock. In the letter to the Corinthians, written much later, this painful experience heads the list of his sufferings which began at this stage.

From Damascus he went, for the first time since his calling, to Jerusalem to meet Peter. "Then after three years I went to Jerusalem to visit Cephas and remained with him fifteen days. But I saw none of the other apostles, except James, the Lord's brother" (Gal. 1:18–19). The innermost reason for his trip would have been his desire to see Jerusalem again, his spiritual homeland. But when "he attempted to join the disciples and they were all afraid of him, for they did not believe that he was a disciple" (Acts

48

9:26), he experienced the typical fate of a convert—he was mistrusted and avoided. Added to this were the many differences in outlook between Saul and the faithful of Jerusalem; the latter had remained in Jerusalem, and were thus understandably more attached to its mores and customs, above all the Temple and the Law, while Saul, having been active abroad, held more independent and cosmopolitan views. Thus the friction was there—even if it did not erupt into the open.

From the statement that after Saul's departure, the Church throughout Judaea, Galilee and Samaria was at peace and grew steadily, one feels clearly how relieved they all were not to have him in their midst. For Saul, this practical though unavowed rejection must have been a bitter disappointment, tempered only by the express designation of his future mission. "When I had returned to Jerusalem and was praying in the temple I fell into a trance and saw him saying to me, 'Make haste and get quickly out of Jerusalem . . . Depart; for I will send you far away to the Gentiles'" (Acts 22:17, 21).

His friends brought him down to Caesarea and sent him off to Tarsus. We don't know how his family reacted to his new way—hardly with enthusiasm. But to Saul none of this meant anything; he had his vision to pursue. The churches in Cilicia certainly owed their existence to his work, the news of which reach Judaea as well.

In the meantime, Greek-speaking Christian Jews, driven from Jerusalem after the martyrdom of Stephen, had founded a church in Syrian Antioch. At first it consisted only of Jews, but soon a number of Greeks joined the community. Among them was Barnabas, a Hellenistic Jew from Cyprus. When, therefore, Barnabas, in need of an able helper, journeyed to Tarsus to induce Saul to join the nascent church in Antioch, he was looking for a man of proven energy and ability.

ANTIOCH ON THE MIGHTY ORONTES

Antioch, about a day's journey by ship from the mouth of the rapid and mighty Orontes, is surrounded on all sides by high mountains. The place where the Orontes breaks through the mountain chain provides a natural connection between the Mediterranean coast and the interior of Asia. The city was founded by Seleucus I in the year 301 BC,

49

Thus I journeyed to Damascus

(Acts 26:12)

Against this majestic setting was to unfold the drama of Paul's conversion: Mount Hermon, its snow-capped head 7,500 feet above sea level towering over the surroundings, such as Paul beheld before the light of the Lord's revelation blinded his eyes.

assumed the prominence of ancient Babylon, and, according to the will of Alexander the Great, was to have become the center of a world empire. After Rome and Alexandria, Antioch was the third largest city of the empire, with over 500,000 inhabitants. Among them, the Syrian element was preponderant, but there was also a large minority of Greek and Macedonian settlers, as well as numerous Persians, Armenians, Nabateans, Arabs and Jews. Praised as the "great and the beautiful", Antioch was famous for its luxury and the mordant wit of its inhabitants, and it had all the brighter and shadier aspects of a cosmopolitan metropolis. It was adorned with magnificent temples, baths, and a street with four rows of columns, which stretched for several miles. Its amphitheater was the largest in the Roman empire. It was noted especially that the city was illuminated at night with lamps: "Day and night differ only in kind of illumination. Industrious hands note no difference, keep right on working and he who feels like it can sing and dance—so that Hephaestus and Aphrodite share the night." Art and culture flourished alongside vice and decadence. The Roman satirist, Juvenal, declared that a river of superstition

50

. . . go to the street called Straight, and inquire . . . for a man of Tarsus named Saul (Acts 9:11)

Now there was a disciple at Damascus named Ananias *(Acts 9:10)*

Blinded on his way to Damascus, Paul was brought by his
companions to an inn in the Straight street, the entrance
to which leads through the gate of the old city (left).
He was healed of his blindness by Ananias at the behest
of Christ. Below, the interior of the chapel standing
on the site of Ananias' house.

... but I went away into Arabia

A stretch of the ancient Nabatean-Roman road (left) linking Damascus and Petra, the capital of the Nabatean kingdom. When Paul retreated into the desert kingdom of the Nabateans, he may have visited Petra (right), famous for its magnificent temples and edifices hewn in the red limestone rock.

and immorality emptied from the Orontes into the Tiber.

Since ancient times the Jews were an especially well-represented community, their number at that period estimated at about 70,000. By virtue of its wealth and prominence, Antioch was understandably a prime goal for an immigrant. Josephus Flavius mentions a wealthy Babylonian Jew, who at the beginning of our era arrived with 500 mounted bowmen and 100 kinfolk in order to settle there. They enjoyed numerous privileges, which were written down on bronze tablets, and which, despite strong opposition, even the emperor Titus did not abolish. In the sources, the beauty of one of the great synagogues is explicitly praised.

The grave of the Maccabean brothers, whose martyrdom apparently took place here, was especially revered. The Jews had close ties with Eretz Israel, which they never ceased to regard as their homeland, and their generous contributions to the temple were sent regularly. A story of the 2nd century AD is indicative of their generosity and devotion to their native land: when Rabbi Akiba came to Antioch

The reconstruction of the facade
of the temple of Ba'al (1st-2nd centuries A.D.)
at Palmyra which Paul might have visited
during his stay in Arabia.

*. . . I was let down in a basket through a window in the wall,
and escaped . . .* (II Corinthians 11:33)

Upon his return to Damascus Paul was met
with open hostility. Unable to leave the city
undetected through one of the guarded
gates, to escape capture he was lowered
down in a basket through a window in the
city wall. Old houses on the city wall
can still be seen in Damascus.

seeking funds for needy students in Judaea, a local
rabbi placed his whole state in Akiba's hands.

Almost nothing remains now of the splendid city
on the Orontes, beyond the great girdle of walls
and a magnificent collection of mosaics. Gone are the
great gateways, colonnaded streets and temples. The
harbor town of Antioch, Seleucia Pieria, is like the
ports of Tarsus, Ephesus and so many others silted
up. The Turkish Antakya of today is a small pro-
vincial town, whose only attraction is its fascinating
landscape.

When Barnabas and Saul's ministry turned Antioch into an important Christian center, the brethren could no longer be regarded as merely another
Jewish sect. It was in Antioch that the disciples
were called "Christians" for the first time (Acts
11:26). The name had an official character and was
given by Roman officials on the analogy of Pom-
pei—Pompeian, Herod—Herodian, and was probably used for entries in the register of the community, especially in connection with the separate burial
society which each community had to have. "Christians", therefore, meant "Men of Christ", designating
a third social group alongside Greeks and Jews.

The narrow alleys of the Old City of Jerusalem recall the streets of that ancient city Paul so often walked.

Sandals, common footwear in the times
of Paul, represented in a 5th century
Byzantine mosaic at Ahias Trias on Cyprus.

THE CONVENTION OF THE APOSTLES

Almost seventeen years had passed since that illu-
minating moment at the gates of Damascus, when
in the year 48 "some men came down from Judaea
and were teaching the brethren, 'Unless you are
circumcised according to the customs of Moses, you
cannot be saved', and when Paul and Barnabas had
no small discussion and debate with them, . . . (they)
were appointed to go up to Jerusalem to the Apostles and the elders about the question" (Acts 15:1–2).
The Jerusalem missionaries were orthodox Jewish-
Christians to whom Saul had long been suspect, for
he attached increasingly less value to the laws
whose observance was for them a matter of course.
Saul's disregard for the sacred laws prompted them
to put to him the decisive question on his position
toward circumcision. Doubtless, their concern was
justified from their point of view. Circumcision is
the sign of the holy covenant and signifies belonging
to the Jewish people. For a child, which already
belongs to Judaism through its Jewish mother, circumcision is merely a sealing of the covenant; but
it is of decisive significance for proselytes, who are
accepted into the Jewish community only after

at Antioch there were prophets and teachers, Barnabas, . . . and Saul *(Acts 13:1)*

Part of an ancient mosaic (left) found at Antioch, representing a scene from Greek mythology. Paul set off on his first missionary journey from Seleucia Pieria (right), the harbor of Antioch at the mouth of the river Orontes.

having committed themselves unreservedly to the covenant (that is what the Hebrew word "Brith" means). The fact that in Paul's time there were many "God-fearers" who had not taken the final step of circumcision is adequate proof that it was a personal sacrifice which many for various reasons were not prepared to make. Thus it was the question of the unity of religion and belonging to the people, as well as the unity of the people and its sacred history, that were the problems at the heart of the discussion. This problem obviously did not exist for the heathen, who could change his religion or adhere to several simultaneously. It has in no way lost its pertinence, since it automatically comes up when a Jew converts to Christianity with the ensuing struggle to render fruitful his Jewish God-given values among Christians, since he too, like Christ, remains of course a Jew.

"I went up into Jerusalem with Barnabas, taking Titus along with me. I went up by revelation; and I laid before them . . . the gospel which I preach among the Gentiles . . . But even Titus, who was with me, was not compelled to be circumcised though he was a Greek" (Gal. 2:2). He makes it unambi-

So, being sent out by the Holy Spirit, they went down to Seleucia (Acts 13:4)

guously clear that he had not been summoned officially before the apostles to account for his actions, but went of his free will, "by revelation", to clear up a problem he considered a matter of conscience. Bringing Titus along was indeed a diplomatic move, destined to test the Jerusalem apostles. In contrast to his opponents, who had to their advantage the solidly based theology of the law which was their mainstay, Saul did not advance any doctrine, but spoke of the gospel. He preached a mission which could be accepted or rejected but which was not subject to discussion, a mission whose basis was the Jesus encountered at Damascus. His stand was that for the mission of bringing the word of redemption and love, circumcision was not necessary.

"When they saw that I had been entrusted with the gospel to the uncircumcised, just as Peter had been entrusted with the gospel to the circumcised . . . and when they perceived the grace that was given to me, James and Cephas and John, who were reputed to be pillars, gave to me and Barnabas the right hand of fellowship, that we should go to the Gentiles and they to the circumcised" (Gal. 2:7–9). This was followed by a recommendation Paul would most gladly comply with—not to forget the poor. This injunction was not so much a question of charity but rather an emphasis on the close ties with the saints in Jerusalem: "Indeed they are in debt to them, for if the Gentiles have come to share in their spiritual blessings, they ought also to be of service to them in material blessings" (Rom. 15:27). The handshake was not merely a friendly gesture, but it had a juridical significance, and was as well symbolic of concord, as it still is in the tribal law of the Beduin. Thus the handshake which followed a common meal, sealed the agreement that Paul's commitment to his mission among the Gentiles could be carried on unhindered. The Gentile-Christian communities became from that moment on the equals of the Jewish-Christian ones.

Peasants, today like in bygone times,
till the rich soil of Seleucia.

Scatter, as from an unextinguished hearth
Ashes and sparks, my words among mankind!
Be through my lips to unawakened earth
The trumpet of prophecy.
(Percy Bysshe Shelley)

3. FIRST MISSIONARY JOURNEY

After the meeting with the apostles in Jerusalem, Paul and Barnabas did not tarry long. They returned to Antioch, bringing along John Mark, Barnabas' cousin, the future author of the Second Gospel. While the faithful were gathered for prayer, the Holy Spirit, speaking by the mouth of one of the "teachers and prophets" who were in the assembly said: "Set apart for me Barnabas and Saul for the work to which I have called them" (Acts 13:1–2). Thereupon the leaders of the Antioch community, according to ancient Jewish patriarchal custom, "laid their hands on them" in blessing "and sent them off". This was to be none other than what is usually known as Paul's first missionary journey beginning in 48 AD.

The goal of the trip was Cyprus: it was the homeland of Barnabas and had commercial links with Tarsus, Cilicia being only 50 miles from the island. Thus from Seleucia, the harbor of Antioch, the missionaries sailed for the capital, Salamis, near modern Famagusta. Its theater, the great gymnasium and the Roman baths still impress the visitor, giving free rein to his imagination of what must have met Paul's eyes upon his arrival.

THE CRADLE OF APHRODITE AND THE STOIC

The island of Cyprus was actually never a transit zone so much as a pond fed by various cultures. As such, Cyprus is not a unique case, but rather a model of the whole Mediterranean region. In addition to the native population, Greeks settled on the island during the great Indo-Aryan migrations, especially after the Trojan war. Near Salamis, a city dating from 1500–1200 BC, Enkoni-Alasia has been dug up. One might call it a "mini-Ugarit" since it is an exact copy of the large city of that name on the Syrian coast. Mediterranean culture, earlier considered a self-contained entity which intensified its contact with the East only as a result of the campaigns of Alexander the Great, had a dynamic oriental component in very ancient times. The much discussed contrast between Hellenism and the Orient simply was not all that sharp. The common pattern and the resulting similarities diverged and developed only much later into individual separate cultures. This explains the many things common to Saul and the Stoic school, which were based not on personal acquaintance or any literary borrowing, but on the

When they had gone through the whole island as far as Paphos

(Acts 13:6)

The coastline of Paphos on Cyprus where, according to a Greek legend, Aphrodite, the goddess of love was "born"—having risen from the foam of the sea nearby.

When they arrived at Salamis, they proclaimed the word of God in the synagogues of the Jews (Acts 13:5)

The gymnasium of Salamis, the thriving harbor where Paul and Barnabas landed on Cyprus beginning their first missionary journey.

same attitude with which they responded to similar stimuli.

Jews settled on the island as early as the 3rd century BC, and maintained close relations with Eretz Israel throughout all times. Through Augustus, Herod received part of the revenues of the copper mines run largely by Jews. In a letter of Agrippa I to Emperor Caligula, Jerusalem is called the capital not only of Judaea but of all Jews including those of Cyprus.

Trade and exporting were brisk, especially of copper, dried fish, salt etc. One specialty was lettuce which, when cooked in salt water, was considered a sedative. The rich collection of terra cotta figurines in the museum of Nicosia shows the unknown artists' considerable gift of observation and an outspoken sense of humor.

"When they [Saul and Barnabas] arrived at Salamis they proclaimed the word of God in the synagogues of the Jews" (Acts 13:5), and then went through the whole island, bound for Paphos. Their route would take them by Kitium, the birthplace of Zeno, the founder of the Stoic school. There the alleged grave of Lazarus, brother of Martha and Mary, is still pointed out to visitors. Lazarus, after being raised from the dead by Jesus in Bethany, went to Kitium and became the first bishop of the city.

At length they came to Paphos. The town was held in high repute because it was the center of the cult of Venus, the Greek goddess Aphrodite. Her oriental counterpart was Astarte, the fertility goddess worshipped under many guises throughout the ancient East. According to a Greek legend, Aphrodite, the celebrated goddess of love, had risen from the foam of the sea nearby. In the rites of spring consecrated to the goddess, pilgrims used to march along the colonnaded parade street, leading from the harbor to the great temple of Aphrodite.

Paphos also had a sizeable Jewish population. One can still see a subterranean tomb with a wide ante-chamber which is dedicated to Solomanii, whose seven sons were martyred for the Jewish faith in 168 BC. It is assumed to be the site of the synagogue where Paul may have preached in Paphos. An ancient legend relates that it was in Paphos that Paul received the "forty stripes save one", supposed to refer to a whip with thirty nine lashes, used by the synagogue in punishment for heresy.

And when they had spoken the word in Perga . . . (Acts 14:25)

Antalia, the ancient Attalia, Perge's once great harbor, where Paul and Barnabas landed after crossing the narrow sea between Cyprus and the coast of present-day Turkey.

Next to a Greek church there is a pillar to which Paul is supposed to have been chained when he received the whipping.

Paphos was the seat of the Roman governor Sergius Paulus, who lived in the elegant residential quarter with a magnificent view of the sea. A Roman villa, marvelously well-preserved, gives an idea of the gracious homes of the patrician society: it contains a total of twenty-two rooms on two floors, grouped around an open colonnaded courtyard, and decorated with wonderful floor mosaics. The mosaics depicted scenes from Greek mythology, showing among others the Triumph of Dionysos, Ganymede carried by an eagle, Pyramus and Thisbe. They are not to be regarded as mere decorations, but may be viewed also as an expression of a religious longing for inner human unity.

Apparently Paul had access to the privileged circles of the city as well. When told of the missionaries' activities, the governor invited them to explain their doctrine to him. Attached to his court there was a magician, a Jew named Bar-Jesus, who naturally did his best "to turn away the proconsul" from the preachers. But Paul, "filled with the Holy Spirit,

68

The great amphitheater of Aspendos, Perge's
sister city, is one of the finest and best
preserved in all Turkey.

70

looked intently at him" and struck Bar-Jesus blind (Acts 13:9). The astounded governor believed and was converted. The demonic power of the eye, encountered occasionally in the East, was characteristic of Paul too. It is at this stage that Saul is first called Paul in the Acts.

From Paphos Paul and his friends sailed across the Pamphylian sea into the Bay of Attalia and up the navigable Kestros River to Perge, which like Tarsus was located but a small distance from the sea. The crossing may have taken them about three days.

PERGE AND THE UPLANDS

Perge has preserved its Hellenistic-Roman character as Paul saw it. The glory of the upper city, certainly as old as the 7th century BC, was its temple of Artemis, the goddess who asserted in a poem by Callimachus (a Hellenistic poet ca. 280 BC), that she loved Perge above all other cities.

Annual festivals were held there. The wealth of the temple, amassed through the pilgrims' offerings, is attested to in Cicero's charges against the Roman legate Verres, whom he accused of having stolen the gold belonging to the goddess as well as having carried away, in broad daylight, all the statues of the city of Aspendos, in collaboration with a native physician.

Below the Acropolis stretched the spacious Hellenistic town, with its long, broad colonnaded streets, its great theater hewn, as such buildings were whenever possible, in the mountainside, and the huge stadium raised on stone vaults.

A lasting testimony to its Hellenistic culture is provided by a famous son of Perge, the mathematician Appollonius, whose book on conic sections is almost as impressive as the discoveries of Keppler and Newton.

It is probable that Paul remained in Perge two months, frequently visiting the surrounding towns. At Aspendos there is a beautiful theater which, in contrast to the Greek theaters where the spectators faced a landscape visible from every seat, is cut off from the outside world and forms a self-contained, architecturally framed space. At Sidé the Jewish community was specifically mentioned in a circular of a Roman consul in 142 BC referring to the renewed alliance with Hasmonean Judaea.

Then they passed through Pisidia, . . . *(Acts 14:24)*

The aqueduct bringing water to Antioch in Pisidia,
the isolated city perched high on the plateau, where Paul
preached after a long and strenuous climb.

The gospel preached by Paul spread amazingly into the wild mountain regions of Cappadocia (eastern Turkey). Seen here are entrances into underground churches constructed by the early Christians as places of refuge from Roman and later Moslem persecutions.

At the end of his stay in Perge, Paul had a painful surprise: John Mark left them and returned to Jerusalem. We do not know the reasons. They may have been connected with the tensions which were later to arise between Paul and Peter; Paul's ideas of bringing the Gospel to the Gentiles may have appeared blasphemous to Mark. Be the reasons as they may, Paul was offended by Mark's abrupt departure.

Paul had set his heart on going to the uplands, and his goal was to reach Antioch in Pisidia. To get there he had to climb a plateau about 3000 feet above sea level.

The journey must have been difficult, since he did not easily forget it, writing later of being "in danger from rivers, dangers from robbers" (2 Cor. 11:26). Why Paul should wish to travel to these isolated, distant districts we do not know. Several scholars have suggested that he may have been suffering from malaria and therefore sought higher altitudes to find relief from the sickness.

Pisidian Antioch was a small isolated town settled by Augustus with a colony of veterans. Fragments of a copy, in Greek and Latin, of the em-

peror's famous testament and the account of his deeds were found in the temple of Augustus in Antioch. Paul may have mused pensively over the text: the "Prince of Peace", as August called himself, belonged to the past. Paul lived under other emperors, among them Claudius who even expelled the Jews from Rome. Paul himself was to have painful experiences with the authorities. Nevertheless he was later to write to the Romans: "Let every person be subject to the governing authorities, for there is no authority except from God" (Rom. 13:1).

As was their custom, they attended synagogue on the Sabbath and "after the reading of the law and the prophets the rulers of the synagogue sent to them saying, 'Brethren, if you have any word of exhortation for the people, say it'" (Acts 13:15). Paul rose solemnly (as a rule the preacher used to sit) "and motioning with his hands", his characteristic gesture, addressed himself both to the Jews and to the "God-fearing". In stirring words he traced the course of Jewish history since the Exodus, culminating with the story of Jesus of Nazareth, who was risen from the dead and "that through this man forgiveness of sins is proclaimed . . ." (Acts 13:38).

The congregation was deeply impressed, and even pagans wished to hear more of the wondrous tidings.

But Paul's success aroused envy and heated exchange ensued with the orthodox members of the synagogue, in the course of which Paul's fiery temperament made him utter the words which were to carry their dramatic impact on history, and to set the Gospel and Christianity on the course it was destined to take. Since they refused to accept the Gospel, "we turn to the Gentiles. For so the Lord commanded us saying, 'I have set you to be a light for the Gentiles, that you may bring salvation to the uttermost parts of the earth'" (Acts 13:47). His words must have fallen on fertile soil, for the Gospel was preached to the pagans throughout the countryside, and by the end of the 6th century the little townlet brought forth 13 bishops.

So "they shook off the dust from their feet and went to Iconium." Ancient Iconium, the present-day Konya, was, then as it still is, an important commercial center with a mixed Jewish and Gentile population.

THE QUAINT ROMANCE

It was a jumble of the most varied social groups, a fertile field for Paul's work. The two missionaries fared here very much as they did in Antioch Pisidia. "The people of the city were divided; some sided with the Jews and some with the apostles" (Acts 14:4). One can imagine the scene of groups engaged in heated discussions, tempers rising, and people even coming to blows. Here it was the latter which led to their departure. But Iconium was the scene of the delightful romance, recorded in the second century apocryphal Acts of Paul and Thekla, which are not historical data but give us an idea of Paul's personal appearance.

The story tells of a meeting between Paul and a young girl of a noble family of Iconium, named Thekla. The word of Paul's deeds had preceded his arrival and a man, Onesiphorus, hearing of Paul's imminent arrival in the city, wished to invite him into his house. He went out to meet him at the gates of the city, but since he had never seen Paul before, he was told to look out for a man answering to the description we have related at the beginning of our story, according to which he identified Paul

immediately. That evening, Paul preached in Onesiphorus' house. Thekla sat at the open window of her adjacent house listening to the impassioned words of the unseen speaker carrying across. His discourse on chastity moved her deeply. Thekla's angry parents brought a charge against Paul for having exerted unwanted influence over their daughter. Paul was imprisoned, but Thekla, bribing his warders, managed to enter his cell in order to listen to his teachings. This defiance brought upon her the wrath of the authorities and she was condemned to the stake, but was saved miraculously by a rain storm. When Paul was finally expelled from the city and went preaching through the countryside, Thekla, disguised as a boy, followed him. When found out, she was again subjected to all kind of torture, but was finally rescued by a lady, daughter of a great and noble Roman family. Ultimately she found refuge in Cilician Seleucia (present-day Selifke) where she devoted the rest of her life to the teaching of the gospel. The small church built over the cave near Selifke where Thekla lived has long since fallen into ruins, but the cave underneath is still pointed out to visitors. The edifying example of

. . . they shook the dust from their feet . . . , and went to Iconium (Acts 13:51)

An ancient Roman bridge on the road to Iconium
(present-day Konya), which Paul might well have crossed
on his way from the Pisidian Antioch.

A chapel in Ma'alula, Syria, commemorating Thekla, the young girl of Iconium who deeply moved by Paul's words left her home and devoted her entire life to the teaching of the Gospel.

Thekla's devotion made her the patron saint of Christian teachers, and many churches in the East as well as in Upper Egypt are dedicated to her.

THE HORRIFIED "GODS" IN LYSTRA

Paul and Barnabas, now for the first time, went to the countryside. The environment here was quite different from what they had experienced thus far; people spoke the local Lycaonic dialect, and only notables and foreigners understood Greek or Latin. They made their way to Lystra, a small townlet which became a Roman colony. There were no Jewish families there. The inhabitants were conservative and observant of the old customs and usages—as people always are in small and out-of-the-way places where little external influence ever penetrates. In the evenings people sat around together, still a favorite pastime in Anatolia, the elders recounting miraculous events of bygone times. One of the ancient legends, which was to have such an unexpected and dramatic bearing upon the apostles' appearance there, was a charming little story connected with the lore of the place. Once, so the story runs, Zeus and Hermes had appeared in the area, in

human form, and asked in vain for shelter. Only an elderly couple, Philemon and Baucis, were ready to take the strangers in, sharing with them the very modest evening meal: milk, cheese and bread. The following morning, the guests, who had in the meantime disclosed their identity, departed taking along with them the old couple. From the top of a mountain overlooking the town, they watched a flood devasting the area; but their own little hut was spared and turned into a temple, while the elderly pair was chosen to become its priests. When their end came, Philemon was transformed into an oak and Baucis into a linden tree, the stumps of which were still shown to people in Roman times.

Strangers rarely ever came to Lystra, so Paul and Barnabas' arrival was of course a sensation, and the whole town led by its priests turned out to welcome them officially. There was a man in Lystra who had been a cripple from birth. Sitting by the road he listened with rapt attention to Paul's preaching. Paul, realizing that the man had faith, looked at him intently and "said in a loud voice, 'Stand upright on your feet.' And he sprang up and walked" (Acts 14:10). In Lystra, stunned and awed, the

Now at Lystra there was a man . . . He listened to Paul speaking (Acts 14:8–9)

Barnabas they called Zeus, and Paul, because he was the chief speaker, they called Hermes (Acts 14:12)

After Paul had performed a miraculous cure of a cripple in Lystra, the inhabitants were convinced that the two visitors—Paul and Barnabas—were gods. Right, the statue of Zeus-Jupiter, a Roman copy of a Greek original made by Phidias in the 5th century B.C. Peasants in Lystra (left), simple and God-fearing folk, now as in the days of Paul, tending their fields.

excited crowds witnessing this wonder reacted according to their views of the supernatural, i.e. they accepted Paul and Barnabas as gods visiting their town in human guise. They imagined in the manifestation of Paul and Barnabas the realization of the ancient legend; Barnabas, who probably had the more imposing presence and was moreover Paul's senior, they regarded as the incarnation of Zeus—while Paul, being the more eloquent of the two apostles, was identified with Hermes, the herald of the Gods. Since the citizens of Lystra spoke Lycaonian, their local vernacular, Paul and Barnabas understood the meaning of the exhilaration which gripped the town only when "the priest of Zeus, whose temple was in front of the city, brought oxen and garlands to the gates and wanted to offer sacrifice" to them. The apostles, horrified, reacting as Jews would against blasphemy, tore their garments crying: "Men, why are you doing this? We also are men, of like nature with you, and bring you good news that you should turn from these vain things to a living God" (Acts 14:13–15). They scarcely managed to restrain the people from offering the sacrifice. But news spread quickly in the environs, the Jews from Iconium arrived and easily managed to reverse the mood of the mob, always very fickle, and by then thoroughly worked up. By a volte-face to which a popular Oriental crowd is so prone, Paul was stoned and narrowly escaped death. Even generations later people recounted these events, but there are no reports of conversions. This is typical of a rural population, deeply rooted in, and holding fiercely on to, its native beliefs, regarding with suspicious distrust any new ideas, which seem to threaten their established order. Christianity took hold slowly, but once established, it was then defended as fanatically as the older faith of the ancestors.

Paul and Barnabas left Lystra the following day, on their way to Derbe, some 30 miles away. There they probably stayed a long time, the only place where they were not persecuted, and made many converts. The area of Derbe has the so-called 1001 churches, ruins of hundreds of partially well-preserved Byzantine churches, which testify to a flourishing Christian life.

They decided, in spite of the danger involved, to return the way they had come and to revisit and encourage the little churches they had founded. So they called again at Lystra, Iconium, Pisidian Antioch and Perge.

To reach their home town, the Syrian Antioch, they took ship at Attalia. Embraced by the mighty wing of the Taurus, with its Mediterranean vegetation and its charming harbor in a niche of a cliff, Attalia leaves an indelible impression. The emperor Hadrian, in whose honor on the occasion of his visit a marble gate flanked by two towers was erected, is supposed to have composed on his deathbed a hymn to Attalia. Yet all this would have been far from Paul's soaring mind, immersed as he was in the single-mindedness of his purpose.

CONFLICT AT ANTIOCH

Great difficulties awaited Paul on his return to Antioch. At the time of the convention of the apostles, occasioned by the question of circumcision, it had been settled that observance of the law as such was not necessary for salvation; belief in Christ was sufficient. But many questions were still open and left unresolved, and in certain situations gradually became acute. In Jerusalem, which was mainly

Jewish-Christian, communal meals posed no problem, since in any case Jewish dietary laws were strictly observed. But conditions were different in the mixed communities where Jewish- and Gentile-Christians lived together. Should the former give up their laws, or the latter be obliged to observe them, or should they refrain from communal meals? When we consider that in everyday life everybody already has his antipathies, for personal or traditional reasons, toward certain foods (how many inhabitants of inland countries do not eat fish, or how many people when abroad seek to order their native dishes), one can understand the disgust felt by someone raised in a Jewish milieu, if he were supposed to eat something "strangled", i.e. the meat of animals killed without the blood being drained, or worse, the blood of it, or of ritually unclean animals. This is not at all a question of ridiculous anachronistic prohibitions, as some Christians might believe, but creates a serious problem which can deeply affect and bedevil the life of an individual who has from childhood grown up with such concepts. This is also a decisive part of the question of how a convert can overcome the problem of "then" and "now". Beyond

this, the problem was one of the principle, whether the observance of these regulations was vital or not. In the abstract, the question had long since been solved indirectly at the convention of the apostles; but on a personal level it kept recurring in everyday life. This was the situation Paul encountered, which was to lead to an open conflict with Peter. When Peter came to Antioch, he at first shared a common table with Gentiles, but when some associates of James (the Lord's "brother") arrived from Jerusalem, he stopped doing so, for fear of giving offense to them. Barnabas did the same. Paul reproached him for that, accusing him of inconsistency: "If you, though a Jew, live like a Gentile and not like a Jew, how can you compel the Gentiles to live like Jews?" (Gal. 2:14). Peter and Barnabas, from a subjective point of view, were certainly no hypocrites; they only reflected the difficulties they were faced with. For Paul, though, the unity of the Jewish and Gentile Christians was at stake. Here was the real Paul, uncompromising in his unswerving devotion to what had become the center of his life—the Lord and the mission entrusted to him. In this light, all other considerations faded into insignificance.

Barnabas . . . sailed away to Cyprus, . . . *(Acts 15:39)*

The monastery of St. Barnabas (left) in
Salamis, Cyprus, honoring the memory of
the apostle, Paul's companion on his first
missionary journey. Right, a monk painting icons.

Having this one goal before his eyes, he had the
courage to oppose, and even challenge Peter. Of
course, Paul was not altogether successful here,
neither do we know Peter's rejoinder. This event
may be connected with James' proposal, when, in
order to resolve the controversy, according to Acts
a sensible compromise was reached, in the form of
resolutions named the Articles of James and em-
bodied in a letter to the communities of Antioch,
Syria and Cilicia: "It has seemed good to the Holy
Spirit and to us to lay upon you no greater burden
than these necessary things: that you abstain from
what has been sacrificed to idols and from blood
and from what is strangled and from unchastity"
(Acts 15:28).

The supremely important point Paul achieved was
that a division had been averted, a split which would
have put severely to test the future development
of the Christian church in its formative years.

Thy shores are empires, changed in all save thee—
Assyria, Greece, Rome, Carthage what are they?
Thy waters washed them power while they were free,
And many a tyrant since . . .

(Lord Byron)

4. SECOND JOURNEY—HELLAS

It was perhaps at this juncture that Paul began to think of his mission as world-wide. But the new churches he had founded on his first journey were especially close to his heart—as the first-born in Christ. Therefore, in the year 49 he made up his mind to revisit them. He asked Barnabas to be his companion again, to "visit the brethren in every city where we proclaimed the word of the Lord and see how they are" (Acts 15:36). Barnabas was willing, but insisted on taking John Mark along as well. Still resentful of Mark's desertion in Pamphylia, Paul would not agree, "and there arose a sharp contention" between the apostles, "so that they separated from each other" (Acts 15:39). Accompanied by John Mark, Barnabas sailed for Cyprus, where his memory is honored by a church and his tomb near Salamis. Paul took for companion Silas, who had been one of the two delegates of the Jerusalem community, entrusted with the delivery of the letter and the explanation of the arguments to the Antioch church.

Paul and Silas traveled by land, and passing through Syria and Cilicia, they "strengthened the churches" wherever they went. In each of these places they told of the decision of the apostles; many new converts' hearts and minds were strengthened, and more found it easy to join the young churches.

In Lystra Paul found a young disciple, Timothy, offspring of a mixed marriage; his mother was Jewish and the father a pagan Greek. Since Paul wanted Timothy to accompany him on his travels, he "circumcised him because of the Jews that were in those places, for they all knew that his father was a Greek" (Acts 16:3), an instructive example of the fact that Paul, far from being inflexible in his principles, was in reality a practical man, loath to hurt sensibilities unnecessarily.

Though originally he set out on his journey eager to visit only those communities he had earlier established, Paul changed his plan en route, because of some inspiration. He and Timothy were moved by the Holy Spirit not to visit the rich Greek cities on the western coast of Asia—Ephesus, Smyrna, Sardis, Pergamum, nor the rich league of cities on the southern coast of the Black Sea, headed by Heracleia. This in spite of the fact that these areas, with their excellent communications network, would have provided him with a rich field for his work. What was in Paul's mind at this juncture? Had he already made up his mind that he must turn west, to Greece and maybe even Rome? At first his route was a little uncertain, and he remained for some time in Galatia, because of poor health and established new communities in the surroundings of Ankara. Traveling through the interior of Asia Minor, it was not until the two reached Troas (just below ancient Troy on the Aegean), that Paul realized clearly that his destination was to be Europe.

A VISION IN TROAS

Troas, once an important city on the Aegean and transit harbor for Macedonia, today but a vast field of ruins spread on alluvial soil, was to become for Paul his great turning point. A visitor to Troas would turn his gaze back into the distant past and muse of ancient Troy not far away, the mighty city of Ilion, which took the Greeks ten years to overthrow. But for Paul, the glorious past of the classical pagan world immortalized in Homer's Iliad, wherein gods and mortals fought side by side, meant very little indeed. For him there was only the living present, life in Jesus Christ. It was in Troas that Paul had the vision which was to mould not only his own destiny, but that of Europe as well: ". . . a man of Macedonia was standing, beseeching him: 'Come over to Macedonia and help us'" (Acts 16:9). The resonance of this vision manifests itself in a dramatic change of style; events are no longer reported in the sober third person: instead—"we sought to go on into Macedonia, concluding that God had called us to preach the gospel to them" (Acts 16:10). One has the impression that the listener and reader and even all of Christendom is drawn into the events. Or was Luke, "the beloved physician" (Col. 4:14), generally identified with the Evangelist and the companion of Paul on his voyages, also with them, as the "we" passages from here on imply?

The party now consisting of Paul, Silas and young Timothy sailed northwest and reached the LUKE island of Samothrace. The island had long been famous as the center of the cult of seafarers' gods. "What Mount Athos is to the Christians, the peak of Samothrace was in the days of heathenism to his Greek ancestors in the same seas" (Conybeare, Meinardus).

Parts of the original mosaic covering the floor of the ancient synagogue of Sardis, a rich and important city on the western coast of Asia. The synagogue is presently extensively reconstructed by an American University archaeological expedition excavating Sardis.

Their call at Samothrace was brief, "and the following day", they took ship to the mainland, landing at Neapolis, today's Kavalla.

Picturesque Neapolis, its old city enthroned on a promontory, was built on two hills, the dip between them spanned by the arches of a Roman aqueduct. It was an important harbor on the great Via Egnatia stretching from Dyrrhachium to Byzantium and linking the Adriatic and Aegean seas. Beyond the Adriatic lay the Via Appia, leading to Rome. The Gospel was destined to make its entry into Europe along these great highways. Landing at Neapolis, Paul proceeded over ten miles to Philippi.

"SEE ME AT PHILIPPI"

Philippi was founded in 357 BC by Philip II of Macedonia, the father of Alexander the Great. It was established on the site of an older settlement called Krenides, after numerous springs ("krene" in Greek) in its vicinity. Owing to the presence of gold mines in the nearby Strymon valley, the town prospered till it became the chief city of the district. Here come to mind Shakespeare's ". . . thou shalt see me at Philippi", the ominous words uttered by

the ghost of the slain Caesar on the eve of the fateful battle, to Brutus, his beloved friend, who had administered "the unkindest cut of all." For it was here, in the year 42 BC, that Brutus and Cassius, the last of the Republicans, who had conspired and slain Julius Caesar, were defeated by the army of Octavianus (the future Emperor Augustus) and Mark Anthony. In gratitude for his victory which was to place the vast imperium in his sole hands, the victory which was to turn the pale young man into Caesar Imperator, Augustus endowed Philippi with the privileged status of a Roman colony.

Now, on the foundations of the mighty empire, on the site of the great dream of Pax Augusta, stood the insignificant-looking Diaspora Jew from Tarsus, commanding no military might—sustained only by the spirit of another humble Jew, Jesus, his Lord. Armed with His word, he stood on the threshold of the greatest conquest in human history. Augustus and Paul—accident or design? For Paul, Augustus was only an historical figure, yet the Pax Augusta—which according to the emperor's will was to outlast the centuries, but was actually declining all too rapidly—ensured a regional unity such as the world

had never known before. This unity, followed by a widespread security, would enable Paul to carry the Word over the vast empire. He encountered the emperor's traces everywhere, not least in the cities which had been founded by him as military colonies, and whose diverse social structure offered ideal points of contact for his pastoral activities.

Thus Philippi, enjoying the double honor of being the origin of both the Roman empire and European Christianity, contains ample proof of both: ruins of a magnificent forum and theater, as well as remains of three basilicas, spread over a large area.

The Jewish community of Philippi was small. Seeking to address the community on the Sabbath as was their custom, Paul and his companions, on the lookout for the synagogue, found a small praying place outside the gate by the riverside. There they addressed the women, who in keeping with the Hellenistic custom not only were not segregated, but enjoyed freedom unheard of in the East. Among them was a business-woman named Lydia, a merchant's widow. She was a dealer in purple cloth, the mainstay of the town's commerce. She was a devout woman in her worship of God, and Paul's words convinced her that his was the true Way. After being baptized with all her household, she insisted on Paul and his companions' lodging in her house.

Luke records yet another incident. According to Luke's narrative, they met a slave girl who possessed the gift of divination. This was exploited by her owners, who made a good income from her sooth-sayings. The girl, apparently attracted by Paul and his companions, followed them, calling out that they were the "servants of the Most High God" (Acts 16:17). Paul was annoyed by what clearly was not a profession of faith, but a distortion of spirit. He cured her by exorcism, but by this act of expelling the spirit he incurred the wrath of her owners, deprived of their generous earnings. They caught Paul and Silas, and dragging them to the market-place, presented the case giving their charges a political insinuation: "These men are Jews and they are disturbing our city. They advocate customs which it is not lawful for us Romans to accept or practice" (Acts 16:20–21). Accusations of this kind had far-reaching implications, and the mob was quite willing to do some Jew-baiting. Brought before the magistrate Paul and Silas were arrested

and treated to what would today be euphemistically called an interrogation, but in those days they had their garments torn off them and were beaten with rods. When the magistrates "had inflicted many blows upon them, they threw them into prison, charging the jailer to keep them safely. Having received this charge, he put them into the inner prison and fastened their feet in the stocks" (Acts 16:23–24). A local tradition identifies an old Roman cistern as the place of the prison, which is divided into two rooms—the outer and inner jail. At midnight, while they were praying and singing hymns, the earth suddenly shook. The gates of the prison sprang open and the fetters fell off. The chief warden expecting a major jail-break drew his sword, ready to take his own life. Paul in his concern to save an innocent man's life called out to him not to harm himself, since they had not fled. Then the warden realized that it must indeed be a different spirit that moved these strange men, who would not snatch at an opportunity when such arose, to save themselves at the cost of another person's life. He wanted to know what prompted this act of self-denial and when told, he "washed their wounds, and . . . was

The Artemis' temple at
Sardis (right). The temple was built in
the Ionic order, distinguishable by its slender
proportions and the volutes on the capitals.
The Ionic capitals gracing the tall columns
are among the most beautiful known.
Below, the reconstructed entrance to the
great 2nd century gymnasium of Sardis.

baptized with all his family." The following day the magistrates instructed the warden to free the prisoners. But Paul, resenting the arbitrary treatment meted out to them, refused to be dismissed in an equally contemptuous manner. "They have beaten us publicly, uncondemned, men who are Roman citizens, and have thrown us into prison; and do they now cast us out secretly?" (Acts 16:37). He demanded that the magistrates accompany them out of prison as an act of public apology. When this was reported to the magistrates, they were appalled at the thought of having publicly abused Roman citizens, and complied with Paul's wishes. Paul and Silas went back to Lydia's house, and after taking leave of her household, departed on their way to Thessalonica.

Philippi was a landmark in Paul's life. Despite persecution, he succeeded in forming the first Christian community in Europe of which he could proudly say: "When I left Macedonia, no church entered into partnership with me in giving and receiving except you only" (Phil. 4:15). The credit was primarily Lydia's for having set up the first Christian women's organization.

Proceeding from Philippi along the Via Egnatia in the direction of Thessalonica, Paul passed through Amphipolis. Founded in the 5th century by the Athenians, it was wrested from them by Philip of Macedonia in 358 BC. To commemorate his victory over the Athenians, a lion monument was erected, a striking landmark which must have surely met Paul's eyes on his journey to Thessalonica. Passing through Apollonia, the three finally came to Thessalonica (modern Salonika), the magnificent harbor city in Macedonia.

Located on a thermal gulf, it had originally been called Thermae, after the hot springs in its vicinity. Thessalonica had actually been founded in 315 BC by one of Alexander the Great's generals, Cassander, and renamed after his wife Thessalonike, Alexander's sister. The city prospered, becoming then as it is now, a great center of commerce and communications, owing to its position at the junction of the Egnatian Way. Under the Romans it was the capital of Macedonia, the seat of the proconsul of the province. As a free city, it had its own city council, which in Paul's days consisted of five "politarchs", the executive officers. The splendid harbor situated at the heart of the Mediterranean basin, was lined with docks. A rich textile industry flourished, specializing in gold-threaded fabrics. The Greek geographer Strabo about 100 BC characterized the city as "populous, easy-going, open to everything new—good or bad." Social differences were considerable; in addition to a well-off upper and a broad middle class, there was in the harbor district a joyless slum quarter, complete with all the shady characters intrinsic to it. Loafers, especially, incurred the wrath of Paul, who thought idleness the root of all major social evil. He was very outspoken about it: "If any one will not work, let him not eat. For we hear that some of you are living in idleness, mere busybodies, not doing any work" (2 Thess. 3:10). There was also a sizeable Jewish community which must have been successful in proselytism, as attested to by the numerous "God-fearers", who later joined Paul's budding community.

As was his custom, Paul began his missionary activity in the synagogue, where he preached on three successive Sabbaths. He argued vehemently, attempting to persuade the Jews that Jesus was indeed the Redeemer, their Messiah. His message would not remain unnoticed: numerous God-fearers, pagans, and a group of women joined him. Such development roused the ire of the orthodox Jewish circles. Led by ruffians, as such demonstrators usually were, an incited mob attacked Jason's house where the missionaries lodged. Not finding the missionaries, they seized Jason and several of the brethren and dragging them before the city authorities, they accused them of giving shelter to men guilty of sedition, since ". . . they are all acting against the decrees of Caesar, saying that there is another king, Jesus" (Acts 17:7). Grave though the accusation was, the politarchs were not unduly impressed; they must have had vast experience in this sort of uproar (and probably much worse rioting) within their multi-racial and multi-societal metropolis, since Jason and his companions were promptly released on bond. But upset, the missionaries left that night for Beroea.

According to the established pattern the debates took place in the synagogue and the preaching to pagans in the outdoor meeting places. In Beroea the Jewish community along with the pagan population was less sophisticated—"more noble than those in

. . . *they went down to Troas. And a vision appeared to Paul in the night* . . . *(Acts 16:8–9)*

The extensive ruins of ancient Troas, just below the Troy immortalized in Homer's Iliad. It was in Troas that Paul had the vision which made him realize the imperative need of carrying the Gospel to Europe.

Thessalonica"—and were thus more receptive to spiritual appeal. They received Paul kindly and with great interest, "examining the scriptures daily to see if these things were so" (Acts 17:11). Many Jews and Greeks, women of high standing as well as men, adhered to the new faith. But unfortunately the pattern would be incomplete without the usual immediate effect such success had on Paul's life: it drove to action again the fanatics of Thessalonica, who came to Beroea trying to incite the crowds. Concerned about Paul's safety and not wishing the trouble come to a head, the brethren accompanied him on his way to the sea, where he set sail for Athens. According to a secondary biblical tradition, Paul traveled by road to Athens, although "he neglected Thessaly, for he was prevented from preaching the word unto them" (Acts 17:15).

That Silas and Timothy were able to stay behind undisturbed points up Paul's towering personality, as indicated by the impact he made on, and the reactions of, his enemies, no less than his friends.

THE PASTOR
The Acts' account of events in Thessalonica is effec-

. . . we made a direct voyage to Samothrace, and the following day to Neapolis . . . *(Acts 16:11)*

Kavalla (left), a port in northern Greece, is the site of ancient Neapolis where Paul first set foot in Europe. The great Roman thoroughfare to the east, the Via Egnatia, terminated at Neapolis. Now as then, fishermen's wives (below) mend nets aboard their small but sturdy craft in the port of picturesque Kavalla.

...and from there to Philippi, which is the leading city of the district of Macedonia *(Acts 16:12)*

The ruins of ancient Philippi
where Paul first preached
the Gospel in Europe.

tively complemented by Paul's letter to the new community, sent from Corinth in the year 50. It is the first of the apostle's writings and also the oldest document of the New Testament. In this letter Paul comes alive, not so much as a theologian or preacher, but as a loving father, concerned about his family, much as a Hassidic rabbi is of his congregation today. Paul and his companions never ceased to work for their living "... with toil and labor we worked night and day, that we might not burden any of you" (II Thess. 3:8). After a long day's work, in the evenings he visited the homes of the faithful, ever ready to comfort and advise, to assist and support when need arose. The relationship was extraordinarily warm on both sides: "... we were gentle among you, like a nurse taking care of her children. So being affectionately desirous of you, we were ready to share with you not only the gospel of God but also our own selves, because you had become very dear to us" (I Thess. 2:7–8). He must have radiated an extremely great force and a very great warmth, this humble, externally undistinguished man, who was moreover a persecuted outcast, expelled from wherever he went. It was

. . . *he put them into the inner prison . . .* *(Acts 16:24)*

Ruins of an ancient church at Philippi,
believed to have stood on the site of the
prison from which Paul was so
dramatically freed.

The statue of Augustus Caesar, the first Roman emperor, whose victory at the battle of Philippi restored peace (*Pax Augusta*) to the vast Roman holdings, thereby preparing the conditions favoring the rapid expansion of Christianity throughout the empire.

this great humility combined with great inner strength and towering intellect, which drew toward him people from all walks of life. Moreover, Paul understood the problems facing converts, especially the inevitable and painful estrangement from kin and clan. He himself was a convert. Separation from one's family, which remained either heathen or Jewish, as the case may be, was an especially weighty matter for a convert in the East, where family relations played (and still do) a major role. Converts to Judaism had had similar difficulties, and the experience of breach from their kin, as well as the acceptance within the new society, was always a painful process. Realizing the difficulties a convert had to contend with, the rabbis admonished severely against taunting them: "You should not oppress proselytes. You should not say to them: 'Yesterday you served idols." With converts to Christianity, the situation, in a somewhat different respect, was much the same. In keeping with the rabbinical injunction, Paul never referred to their lives prior to conversion, instead expressly called them "brethren beloved by God." He understood that exposed to the various external and emotional pressures, as well *we went outside the gate to the riverside, . . . we sat down and spoke to the women who had come together* (Acts 16:13)

The river Gangites where, according to tradition, Lydia from Thyatira, the "seller of purple goods", was baptized by Paul. She and her entire household became Paul's first converts at Philippi.

as to the feeling of isolation and loneliness, they ran the risk of relapsing into their past, not being equal to coping with the difficulties. As long as Paul was with them, they were elated, and, through his moral support, on firm ground, but after his departure they felt doubly orphaned. Helping them to overcome their difficulties Paul saw as a prime task, to be accomplished exclusively by personal involvement. In this light we can understand that though about to set out on a long journey, Paul found time to concern himself with what was after all a small community. And no matter how small, each community was his child to be reared, tended, strengthened and above all cherished. Therefore his letters to them were of such significance as to make all other tasks secondary. He did not make light of the pressures they had to contend with: "You yourselves know that this is to be our lot" (I Thess. 3:3). But he could and did lighten the burden of isolation, by constant and forceful reassurance that he and the brethren formed an inseparable community in the Lord.

In addition to individual conversions, reference is repeatedly made to the baptism of some person together with his household. According to the Oriental mentality the father, or after his death the matron, can take action on behalf of the family. Since Paul was often in a place a short time, only the briefest instruction could precede baptism. It is remarkable how quickly small communities left on their own grouped around a family, such as that of Lydia in Philippi, Aquila and Priscilla in Corinth. Christian hospitality became an important part in the religious life, especially for the "family-liturgy". Moreover Paul exhorted the converts "to stand firm and hold to the tradition which you were taught by us, either by word of mouth or by letter" (II Thess. 2:15) or he sent his collaborators "to establish you in your faith and to exhort you."

THE CITY OF PERICLES

According to an old proverb, Athens is for the world what spring is for the earth and the stars for the heavens. Humanity, learning, religion, justice and laws, according to Cicero, spread throughout the whole world from Athens; and despite its political collapse and subsequent intellectual decline, the illustrious name of ancient Greece, evoking the spirit of

Now when they had passed through Amphipolis and Apollonia

(Acts 17:1)

The lion monument set up in the 4th century
B.C. must have been seen by
Paul as he was proceeding along the Via
Egnatia, passing through Apollonia (left)
in the direction of Thessalonica.

beauty, aesthetics, philosophy and science, shines forth exclusively through the authority and luster of that city. Although the Athens visited by Paul was but a shadow of its former glory, it was still, outwardly at least, the "violet crowned city of Pericles", the intellectual capital of Greece, distinguished by its splendid monuments.

Standing on the rock in the heart of the Acropolis in the late afternoon, one is enchanted by the sight of the soft, golden light of the setting sun reflected by the marble temples: the Parthenon, the temple of the goddess Athena Parthenos (the virgin), the Erectheion, the Propylaea—those perfect examples of the beauty of Greek architecture. Below glows the white temple (called the Theseum) of Hephaestus, the limping god of fire and smithery. Musing leisurely on the Acropolis, one's eyes encompass the vast panorama of the sprawling, cross-shaped and very restless city, with the steep Lycabettus and the dark silhouette of the honey-bearing Hymettus looming on its edge. The dark stones on the rocky "hill of Ares", the Areopagus, draw the eyes of the beholder. In classical times, the supreme court of Athens sat here. Traces of altars, seats and stair-

cases leading up to the Areopagus are still in evidence. Down in the west glitters the Bay of Phaleron and the harbor of Piraeus, its countless ships struck by the last rays of the sun. Down the slope, spreads the theater of Dionysus, restored in the Hellenistic period, its places of honor decorated with lions and satyrs, its stage of magnificent decor. Here the great dramatists had been presented: Aeschylus showed in "The Persians" that one must have sympathy for one's enemy; Sophocles gave his Oedipus, the external exile, hope of yet coming to rest in Athens, and made his Antigone utter the famous words: "I am here not to join in hating but to join in loving." Euripides presented the great figures of history reduced to man-size, and in human warmth. There "the merry Greek, tart Aristophanes" (Ben Johnson) subjected state and society to biting merciless criticism, and Menader amiably poked fun at man, his vanities and foibles.

But now the island of Rhodes had supplanted Athens as the real cultural center of Greece. Cicero himself, the paragon of orators, the illustrious poet Horace, and indeed even Tiberius himself, in his youth, had all studied philosophy and oratory on Rhodes. The Athenians' philosophy in Paul's time was certainly sophisticated, but amounted to little more than intellectual acrobatics.

Paul would have seen also some later embellishments—the Roman Forum, which we can still behold, as well as many buildings on the Agora, including the famous Painted Stoa (portico) from which the disciples of Zeno derive their name. Being too poor to rent a hall, Zeno had taught in that Stoa, hence his school's name—Stoic. The joy the pure beauty of these monuments evoke in the soul of a beholder was alien to Paul—his emotion was contrary to ours. To him they were not the fruit of man's soaring genius in his quest for perfection, but shrines of false gods, and thus, in his eyes, the embodiment of evil. All this display was for him blasphemy, the violation of the Law of God.

PHILOSOPHERS WISE AND OTHERWISE

Paul felt very lonely upon his arrival in Athens. He begged the friends who had come with him to the coast to send Silas and Timothy to him as soon as possible. Where he lodged we do not know, but he passed his time as usual preaching in the synagogue.

108

The Jewish community was small. We know only of several funerary inscriptions relating to women of Oriental origin. In Plutarch's round-table talks, an Athenian refers favorably to the Jewish religion, and thus it may be presumed that he may have known Jews living in his city.

The Athenian stands out as a very distinct type among his neighbors of the Mediterranean: cheerful, happy-go-lucky, making light of adversity, witty and intelligent, he has an inquisitive, restless spirit constantly on the lookout for news, gossip or idle chatter and given to dialectics on any unproven idea. His piety and reverence for his multifarious gods conformed dutifully to tradition but had a generous dose of scepticism thrown in for good measure. Enlightened and sophisticated, arguing endlessly about human destiny, and inclined to sophism, admirably expressed in Pilate's famous words: "What is truth?" (John 18:38), the Athenian was an adversary such as Paul had never encountered before.

The Jews had feelings of inferiority in relation to the Athenians. The Talmud relates a story of a rabbi who challenged the elders of Athens to a dispute and defeated them. In the Midrash on Lamentations there is a tendency "to emphasize the superior wit and wisdom of the Jerusalem Jews over the Athenians" for which reason many stories began with the sentence: "An Athenian came to Jerusalem. . . ."

Athenians throughout the ages passed much of their waking time outdoors; the ancients tended to spend it in the Agora, which besides housing the offices, was also the commercial center of the city. The old comic poet Eubolus declared with a tongue-in-cheek seriousness that one could find anything for sale there: figs, turnips, witnesses, chickpeas, myrtle, law-suits, porridge, roses, indictments, lambs and waterclocks. Paul in Athens did as the Athenians did—so we find Paul in the Agora (Perowne).

It was . . . "some of the Epicurean and Stoic philosophers" (Acts 17:18) that Paul met and addressed in Athens. The Epicureans' serene equanimity and their deities' non-involvement in human affairs was a revolting blasphemy for Paul, steeped as he was in his Jewish heritage, wherein all and every single aspect of life is of God's provenance and His manifestation. That he was acquainted with Stoicism

Via Egnatia, the great Roman thoroughfare, which linked the Adriatic and Aegean seas. Along this road trod Paul westward, on his way from Philippi to Thessalonica.

from his days in Tarsus we have already seen. However there is a deep incompatibility between Paul and the Stoics in relation to the belief in a personal God and in an "I-Thou" relationship between God and man. The fundamental contrast between the life without Christ and the life in Christ is the root of Paul's existence. The ever curious Athenians, perpetually in quest of new ideas, "the Epicurean and Stoic philosophers . . . brought him (Paul) to the Areopagus, saying, 'May we know what this new teaching is which you present?'" (Acts 17:18–19). The ensuing scene is a masterly display of Paul's intellectual bravura. Drawing on their own sources, and quoting their own poets, Paul expounded brilliantly the idea of a single and indivisible deity. He took as his point of departure "an altar" he had seen, bearing an "inscription, 'To an unknown God." "What therefore you worship as unknown, this I proclaim to you." This God "does not live in shrines made by man (such as surround them), nor is he served by human hands, as though he needed anything (such as the offerings abounding on the altars) since he himself gives to all men life and breath and everything." "Yet he is not far from each of us,

for 'In him we live and move and have our being', as even some of your poets have said, (quoting the poet Aratus) 'For we are indeed his offspring'" (Acts 17:23–28). So far, so good—this the philosophers could accept—but that was not the purpose for which Paul had taken the trouble to reach Athens. His outward conformity, reflected in his ability to meet his listeners on seemingly common ground, was one of his principles, provided it did not conflict with any of his others. So now he continued, emphasizing each word: "The time of ignorance God overlooked, but now he commands all men everywhere to repent, because he has fixed a day on which he will judge the world . . ." (Acts 17:30–31). The idea of sin and repentance self-understood for a Jew or Christian was indeed very strange to the Greeks: if their acts displeased the gods for one or another reason, the obvious logical course to take was to change one's behavior accordingly. But to repent? They were puzzled. But there was more to come. God "will judge the world . . . by a man whom he has appointed and of this he has given assurance to all men by raising him from the dead" (Acts 17:31). This unheard-of statement on resur-

110

. . . they came to Thessalonica, where there was a synagogue of the Jews *(Acts 17:1)*

An old synagogue in Thessalonica, where Paul found a thriving Jewish community to which he addressed himself.

rection stretched the bewildered philosophers' patience and credibility too far. The Epicureans—reared upon Epicurus' famous dictum: ". . . Death, the king of terrors, is nothing to us, because as long as we exist Death is not present, and when Death comes, we are no more"—were mocking. They refused to listen to any more of this absurdity, "but others", presumably some of the Stoics, "said, 'We will hear you again about this'" (Acts 17:32). Broad-minded and understandably tolerant, it would not cross the Athenians' mind to ill-treat the man for his strange ideas; but precisely for the same reason he did not make much headway in conversions either. "Some men joined him and believed, among them Dionysius the Areopagite and a woman Damaris and others with them" (Acts 17:34). Paul's entry into the metropolis of Hellenism and his great speech to the "men of Athens" must have represented a high point for the author of the Acts. But Paul is presented in idealized fashion here, while the reality is much more prosaic.

THE FORLORN WELL
Where could one find Paul in Athens? Under the

Areopagus, near the ruins of the church of Dionysius Areopagita, there is, a few feet behind the apse, a well, now completely filled up. According to a late legend of the 17th century, after the conversion of Dionysius, who was a member of the Areopagus itself, there was an outcry among the people, and this well served Paul as a hiding place for a while. Historically, the place is of course of none such thing, but the dry well may be regarded as a symbol of the barrenness of Paul's stay in Athens. Paul wrote the Athenians no letters; his only mention of Athens (I Thess. 3:11) is that he was alone there. This blocked-up well is therefore a symbol in yet another respect that borders on the tragic: the peculiar lack in the entire Greco-Oriental world of memorial sites for Paul; few modern churches are consecrated in his name; not a single Greek monastery bears his name. Only in Patmos and in Aigialia do people point out a few relics connected with him. In the main centers of his missionary activity, his disciples or other saints are revered: in Athens—Dionysius, in Salonika—Demetrius, on Crete—Titus, on Cyprus—Barnabas. Even in Antioch, Peter is recalled by a grotto church in which he is supposed

113

One of the principal monuments of Thessalonica, the Arch of Galerius (4th century A.D.). Galerius, one of the four emperors who ruled the empire at the time was stationed on the banks of the Danube to safeguard the Illyrian provinces whose center was Thessalonica.

to have preached. In Jerusalem only a lateral altar in the Church of the Flagellation recalls his capture with a picture by Barberis. The reasons for this strange omission are not easily understood, and the various opinions professed by researchers can, in the main, be only speculative. The saints mentioned above, with the exception of Barnabas, were all Greeks, natives of, and rooted in, the places where they reared and ministered their fledgling Christian communities. But Paul's personality was complex: a Jew, whose vernacular was Greek and citizenship Roman, he was a cosmopolitan, who actually did not belong to any one place, but to the world at large. His stay with the newly formed communities was usually brief—driven by an intense inner sense of mission, he raced like a whirlwind from place to place—while his disciples built up the communities slowly and painstakingly. Also, in a country with a strong cultic orientation, his uncompromising, spiritual theology, with his abhorrence of any graven image, would have difficulty in finding receptive religious soil. Rome, where he was later to suffer his martyrdom which provided grounds for numerous memorial sites, the situation was dif-

ferent. Rome was a cosmopolitan city, the capital of the then known world; there Paul, the citizen of the world, belonged. Thus, the largely unknown well in Athens is perhaps the most moving site there, connected, however loosely, with Paul, the Paul who conquered the world for his Lord, but as a human being remained as lonely as the forlorn well.

"TWIN-SEA'D CORINTH"

From Athens Paul went to Corinth which became his field of activity for a year and a half (ca. 49/50–52/53). Overshadowed by the isolated and towering citadel of Acrocorinth with its famous temple of Aphrodite, the twin-harbored city, thanks to its favorable position on the isthmus, is located on both the Aegean and Adriatic seas, with a harbor on each of them. In order to avoid the storm-haunted capes at the southern tip of Greece, ships were transported by a slipway called "diolkos" across the isthmus, from one sea to the other. The four mile long canal, considered by Alexander the Great and begun by Nero's engineers, was opened only at the end of the 19th century.

After the destruction of Corinth suffered at the hands of the Romans in 146 BC, the city was quickly rebuilt by Julius Caesar with appropriate splendor, surpassing even Athens, since it became the seat of the governor of the province of Achaia. A marble-paved, colonnaded road, leading from the western harbor and ending in the center of the city, the Agora, the Stoa and the archaic temple of Apollo, still convey the impression it must have made on Paul. The Greek geographer Strabo thus describes the atmosphere of the great city: "Corinth is called wealthy because of its atmosphere, for the celebrations of the Isthmian Games brought in crowds; the sanctuary of Aphrodite was so wealthy that it possessed as slaves more than one thousand courtesans; the city was thronged and enriched, for the sailors spent their money easily, and on that account the proverb says: 'not for every man is the voyage to Corinth'."

Corinth's main export consisted of bronzes and pottery, the distinctive forms and beauty of the latter making the Corinthian vase a coveted status symbol through the centuries. The city was also famous for its architecture, giving the name to the third order of the Greek style—namely the Corin-

. . . the word of God was proclaimed by Paul at Beroea also, . . .

(Acts 17:13)

Frescoes in the 14th century Byzantine church
in Beroea, where Paul stopped and preached
in the local synagogue. From the nearby
coast Paul boarded a coasting
vessel bound for Athens.

. . . at Athens, his spirit was provoked within him as he saw that the city was full of idols

(Acts 17 : 16)

View of the Acropolis in Athens, the site of the most famous masterpieces of architectural art. The ruins of the lofty marble temples—monuments raised by man's soaring genius—still radiate the air of past glory.

thian (after the Ionic and Doric) with its distinctive foliated capitals.

Yet it is not difficult to understand the fascination emanating from this colorful, multi-lingual creation, with its amalgam of races and cultures, embraced by the blue, sparkling waters of the Adriatic and the Aegean—Horace's "twin-sea'd Corinth". Its motley, varied population ranged from Roman aristocrats to the homeless dispossessed poor. It was said that in the midst of this fabulously rich city the poorest gathered around bread-sellers to pick up bread-crumbs from the ground.

IN SEARCH OF "A MAN"

In addition to the cult of Aphrodite and Apollo, various Oriental cults thrived. Miracle-makers, mendicant priests, especially the latter, plied their trade, reducing the status of religion to common trickery and vulgar entertainment. A wall painting in the Villa Pamphili in Rome depicts several mendicant priests dancing around a picture of a god, while another stands holding out his hat to onlookers to toss in their offerings. It was in Corinth that Diogenes walked out into the market place in broad

118

So Paul, standing in the middle of the Areopagus, said: 'Men of Athens, . . . this I proclaim to you. The God who made the world and everything in it, . . . does not live in shrines made by man, . . . (Acts 17:22–24)

The tablet with the transcript of Paul's impassioned speech on the Areopagus, delivered at the request of some of the Stoic and Epicurean philosophers in Athens.

daylight, a lighted lantern in his hand, looking for a "man". Paul might have walked past his grave, decorated with a statue of a dog; he might have felt a kindred affection and sympathy for this man, who in times of excessive civilization and opulence, had a barrel for a home. His only personal possession, a water-cup, he discarded as well when he saw a child drinking from cupped hands, claiming that all a man really needed to retain his soul was self-sufficiency. Paul's attitude to earthly possessions was similar, but his aim was not self-sufficiency but a communion of brothers and sisters united in love of the Lord and of man. Indeed, if for some Corinth was the pinacle of earthly bliss, for Paul it was a challenge.

The Jewish community, the most important in Greece, had its synagogue on the outskirts of the city. A pillar with three "menorahs" (seven-branched candelabras), a "lulav" (palm frond) and "ethrog" (citron), and bearing an inscription reading "(Syn)agogue of the Hebr(ews)", was found in the excavation of the city. Corinthian copper was used for the gates of the temple in Jerusalem. After his victory in the Galilee (66 AD) Vespasian sent 6,000 young Jewish prisoners of war to forced labor in the construction of the canal.

On arrival, looking as usual for his co-religionists, Paul had the good fortune to meet a Jewish-Christian couple called Aquila and Priscilla. Originally of Pontus, they had migrated to Rome, from which they were subsequently expelled in 49 AD by the edict of the Emperor Claudius. Their presence in Corinth at the time of Paul's visit was a boon from heaven for him: they were able to tell him of the already established community in Rome. Aquila and Priscilla were also "by trade ... tentmakers, ... and because he was of the same trade, he (Paul) stayed with them" (Acts 18:3), a happy coincidence indeed, which provided him with a home and livelihood, as well as the warm companionship of established and experienced adherents of the Way. Another cheering experience was the long waited arrival of Silas and Timothy; they carried good news of the steadfastness of the Thessalonian converts. The news from the Thessalonian brethren moved Paul to write the first letter to the Thessalonians, the first document of the New Testament (52 AD).

Paul's stay in Corinth was singularly fruitful. He first preached in the synagogue, and performed some conversions—the most notable convert, Crispus, was the head of the synagogue. These conversions obviously brought opposition in their wake and made Paul leave the synagogue altogether. Turning to the Gentiles, he set up his community in the house of the God-fearing Justus.

During Paul's stay in Corinth a new proconsul was appointed—Junius Annaeus Gallio was his name. He was the brother of the famous Roman Stoic philosopher Seneca. An inscription found at Delphi reproduces a letter of the Emperor Claudius, in which reference is made to Gallio as the proconsul of Achaia (51–52 AD).

Hoping that the new governor, Gallio, might be more inclined to proceed against Paul, the heads of the synagogue brought him to the basilica of the court before the proconsular "bema", the remnants of which can still be seen today. Paul was accused of "persuading men to worship God contrary to the law." The charge sounded absurd to Roman ears, since the Romans were as a rule little concerned with particulars of worship. Gallio was now bothered with matters as trifling as "questions about

But some men joined him and believed, among them Dionysius the Aeropagite . . . *(Acts 17:34)*

Ruins of the church of Dionysius Areopagita
on the Areopagus, named after one
of the few converts Paul made during
his stay in Athens.

words and names and your own law." Just when Paul opened his mouth to reply, Gallio cut the proceedings short: "If it were a matter of wrong-doing or vicious crime, I should have reason to bear with you . . .", but since the now thoroughly annoyed Stoic was troubled with theological defini-tions, he contemptuously "refuse[d] to be a judge of these things. And he drove them from the tri-bunal." The Greeks then "seized Sosthenes, the ruler of the synagogue and beat him in front of the tribu-nal", while the bored and scornful proconsul "paid no attention to this" (Acts 18:12–17).

After this incident, Paul stayed on in Corinth "many days longer" and then accompanied by Pri-scilla and Aquila left the city by way of the eastern port Cenchrea. There he cut off his hair, in order to fulfill a Nazarite vow, which obliged him also to abstain from wine for 30 days, to observe the pre-scriptions of purity and to bring his hair as an offering to the Temple. What the nature of the vow was we do not know. He also wished to go to Jerusalem for the Feast of Weeks (or first-fruits), one of the three annual pilgrimage festivals.

The ship sailed to Ephesus. There, Paul stayed only a few days, which included a Sabbath, and on which, as was his custom, he went to the syna-gogue. His discourse there must have aroused con-siderable interest, for he was asked to stay longer. Paul declined, since he wished to spend the feast in Jerusalem and fulfill his vow. "But taking leave of them" he promised ". . . to return . . . if God wills" (Acts 18:20). Leaving his friends, Priscilla and Aquila in Ephesus, he sailed to Caesarea. He then "went up and greeted the church" in Jerusalem. Very soon, however, he returned to Syrian Antioch, which had become his home base (52–53 AD).

JEW AND MISSIONARY

When we survey Paul's activities thus far, the first thing that strikes us are the great distances he covered in such a comparatively short time. He was interested in the extent of the Roman world only so far as it meant the possibility of bringing the message of Christ to its furthermost corners. Traveling extensively through this variegated and fascinating world, he gained knowledge and experi-ence. But the resplendent culture and beauty of the Aegean cities, then at their zenith, and later the

After this he left Athens and went to Corinth *(Acts 18:1)*

Acrocorinth (left), the isolated limestone
rock towering 1500 feet over Corinth.
The great city was especially favored by its
unique position on the isthmus (below),
commanding approach to both the Aegean
and Adriatic seas.

overwhelming grandeur of Rome itself, all left this seasoned traveler cold and unimpressed. His eyes beheld only the vision of his Lord, and the goal set before him in the encounter at the gates of Damascus. All the power of his intellect was directed to the realization of this one goal, and the passionate heart of this lonely man was emblazoned with the only real wisdom—the wisdom of love. "And if I have prophetic powers, and understand all mysteries and all knowledge, and if I have all faith, so as to remove mountains, but have not love, I am nothing" (I Cor. 13:2). This beautiful lyric contains the essence of Paul's teaching.

What had Paul achieved? His infant churches survived the vicissitudes of the first turbulent years. True, some of the churches were assailed by a variety of problems, some so trivial that they might seem irrelevant, but precisely these questions would have been of prime importance to the community of converts: should Christians accept invitations to the homes of pagans and eat with them? Should they eat meat left over from sacrificial rites and then sold on the market? Should a Christian have recourse to heathen courts? Should women have

In the shadow of its rocky citadel lay the city of Corinth on two levels. On the upper one stood the 6th century B.C. temple of Apollo, of which seven lofty columns still bear witness to its greatness. The temple was still standing in Paul's time, drawing thousands of worshippers.

126

And you shall make a lampstand of pure gold . . . and there shall be six branches going out of its sides *(Exodus 25:31–32)*

Commonly used as a decorative motif in Jewish synagogues, the *menorah* (seven-branched candelabrum) graces the columns of an ancient synagogue in Ostia, and was also found in Corinth.

their heads covered during divine service in accordance with the prevailing Greco-Roman mores? These are but a few. Paul gave his answers in the light of Jesus. Where questions of faith were concerned, he was rigid; in other matters he let things take their own course and, in particular, did not build up any casuistic system.

In Corinth the issues were, in addition, complicated by sectarian rivalry within the church. Groups formed, some regarding themselves on a higher spiritual plane than Paul. "I belong to Paul", "I belong to Apollos", "I belong to Cephas." Paul would have none of it, and his quick wit cuts sharply through these pretenses: "Is Christ divided?" (I Cor. 1:12). "What do you wish? Shall I come to you with a rod or with love in a spirit of gentleness?" (I Cor. 4:21).

Paul always felt and considered himself a Jew. His reaction in Athens, where "his spirit was provoked within him as he saw that the city was full of idols" (Acts 17:16) was typical of him. Throughout his life, in his teachings and writings, he remained faithful to his Jewish heritage. In his preaching he followed the structure of synagogue usage which

129

began with a quotation from the Old Testament, and then he traced the historical road to salvation, at that point proclaiming Jesus, crucified and resurrected, as the Messiah. In his interpretations of the Scriptures, he used the methods he had learnt from Gamaliel. He used the same method when addressing the heathen, so that one may ask oneself whether his listeners really always understood him. In his letter to the Romans, he painted a dark picture of the immorality of the heathen, which scarcely corresponds to reality, but for a long time significantly influenced Christian opinion.

It is interesting to consider the correlation between Judaism and Paul's theological orientation. The discovery of the priceless Scripture Scrolls found at Qumran, belonging to a Jewish sect, the Essenes, Paul's contemporaries who lived in the area of the Dead Sea, was a sensation that stirred not only the theological Jewish and Christian world, but also many laymen. Here, for the first time, were documents from the time of Jesus, calling for comparison with the New Testament. Therefore the question of evaluating the reciprocal relationship of Paul and the Essenes is a natural one. We do not know if he was personally acquainted with this community or had heard of it. But since they both emerged from a Jewish background, there are, of course, many similarities which originated independently of each other. On the other hand, one must note the differences which were conditioned by the special milieu in which each of them lived. Let us take as an example of an interesting juxtaposition of Scripture interpretation the famous phrase of the prophet Habakkuk: "The righteous shall live by his faith" (2:4). It refers to the people which despite its enemies will survive through its trust in God. According to the Essenes, "this concerns all those who observe the Law in the House of Judah, whom God will deliver from the House of Judgment because of their suffering (studying the Torah) and because of their faith in the Teacher of Righteousness" (Hab. Commentary 8:12). For Paul it contains the answer to all the questions of humanity: "He who through faith (in Jesus Christ) is righteous shall live" (Rom. 1:17). Paul, though, makes no mention of the Law, which is of great importance for the Essenes.

The Qumran museum in Jerusalem, the Shrine of

Part of the Israel Museum in Jerusalem,
the Shrine of the Book was constructed to
house the Dead Sea Scrolls, the oldest Bible
manuscripts ever found.

the Book, has the form of the original artifact—the shape of the jar wherein the priceless manuscripts were found. Its shining white surface stands out in sharp contrast to the black wall opposite it, and is thus a symbol of the struggle of the Sons of Light against the Sons of Darkness, a subject to which one of the preserved manuscripts is devoted. The Oriental man in general had a definite feeling that human life was adversely influenced by dark "principalities and powers"; according to Qumran, they would be defeated in an eschatological battle by the Sons of Light; according to Paul, they were already divested of their power by Jesus, and would be finally quashed by his appearance at the Second Coming.

Who were his listeners? Paul addressed himself to all—Greek philosophers, Jewish sages, wealthy "God-fearers"—but above all to the lowly, oppressed, poor and dispossessed multitudes, the "little people." Among the latter, the slaves were especially responsive. Their condition differed from nation to nation. A Jewish slave fared best: the Law expressly and strictly forbade mistreatment of a slave in any way whatsoever, for "you shall remember that you were a slave in the land of Egypt" (Deut. 15:12). He had to be released in the jubilee year, and it was incumbent on Jewish communities to redeem their members who had been taken into slavery by pagans. In Rome the slave grew up in the family, where he received his education, and in the imperial period was often the teacher and mentor of his master's children. He enjoyed liberties his Greek counterpart was never accorded. It was the Greek slave's lot which was the hardest: a faceless shadow, deprived of any individuality, in total dependence on his master's whim. These sorry human beings were the people Paul concerned himself with most. They were understandably receptive to his message: "There is neither Jew nor Greek, there is neither slave nor free, there is neither male nor female, for you are all one in Jesus Christ" (Gal. 3:28). It would awaken the long forgotten hope of a better world. Hasn't this same Christ proclaimed that "Blessed are you poor, for yours is the kingdom of God" (Luke 6:20)?

How close to Paul's heart these "little people" were is best seen in the charming, warm and personal letter, which he wrote from his captivity in Ephesus, to Philemon, a wealthy Christian in Colossae whose slave, Onesimus, had run away, probably in order to escape punishment for some misdeed. The slave knew Paul well from his master's house, and thus fled to Paul for protection. Paul sent him back with a letter—"I, Paul, an ambassador and now a prisoner also for Christ Jesus—I appeal to you for my child, Onesimus, whose father I have become in my imprisonment. Perhaps this is why he was parted from you for a while, that you might have him back for ever, no longer as a slave but . . . as a beloved brother . . . So if you consider me your partner, receive him as you would receive me. If he has wronged you at all, or owes you anything, charge that to my account. I, Paul, write this with my own hand, I will repay it . . ." (Philemon: 9, 12, 15–19).

This letter, more than others, permits a glimpse into the soul of this lonely and reserved man, to reveal a wealth of love, warmth and compassion. He was a man, who actually lived what he preached.

Paul broke through the boundaries of class distinction and discrimination, which persisted also in regard to "freemen": the slaves were bought with a price, "the man Christ Jesus . . . gave himself as a ransom for all" (I Tim. 2:6). The all important con-

cept of redemption comes to us from the world of the slaves.

What was his listeners' reaction to his words? He himself had characterized it shrewdly: "Jews demand signs and Greeks seek wisdom, but we preach Christ crucified, a stumbling block to Jews and folly to Gentiles" (I Cor. 1:22). He did not excel in eloquence—others surpassed him. But Paul knew the power of the spoken word, well aware of the danger that listeners might be carried away by the flow of oratory (so beloved in the Greco-Roman world!) and lose sight of the essence and message it carried.

Paul was a serious man. In this he was in no way exceptional in the Oriental milieu which lacked the quick wit and withering repartee of the Greeks. According to the rules of Qumran, he who laughed aloud at something foolish was punished (7:14). Paul, a Jewish scholar, forbids "silly talk" and "levity" to Christians (Eph. 5:4). This intense earnestness was a salient characteristic of his personality, which remained totally impervious to the influences of the Hellenistic-Roman world, of which satire, comedy and humor were an intrinsic feature.

A jar in which the Dead Sea scrolls were found in the caves of Qumran. The manuscripts were written by scribes of a Jewish sect, the Essenes, who were Paul's contemporaries.

When told that Herod, suspecting treason in his household, did not even spare the life of his son, Augustus is credited with a remark to the effect that he would rather be a pig (which the Jews abhorred) than a son in Herod's house. Such witticism would have been inconceivable for Paul, though he wielded irony and sarcasm effectively; he once graced the high-priest with the epithet of a "white-washed wall" (Acts 23:3).

In a patriarchal society, where conformity is a virtue and where life is strictly governed by tradition, little value is accorded to independence of spirit. But Paul, like his Lord and the prophets, had the courage of his convictions: "I am not ashamed of the gospel" (Rom. 1:16) and "I will boast of the things that show my weakness' (II Cor. 11:30). And although it made him a man "set apart", it also gave him the strength to bear the most unbearable of human burdens—the burden of loneliness.

5. THIRD MISSIONARY JOURNEY

Paul returned to Antioch, the center of his missions. One should expect the travel-weary man to enjoy for a while at least the warm companionship of the big and prospering community of brethren, well established in the Christian faith. But this was not the case. It would seem that through the years of absence, Paul became estranged from the community, whether through default of keeping up the ties with them, or whether because his opponents there might have utilized his absence to create a mood of coolness toward him—the fact remains that Paul did not tarry in Antioch. When he wrote to the Philippians "you . . . yourselves know that in the beginning of the gospel, when I left Macedonia, no church entered into partnership with me in giving and receiving except you only" (4:15), it sounded like a veiled reproach to his former community, which, after setting out on his third journey in the spring 53, he was never to see again.

So began what is known as the Third Missionary Journey. His immediate destination was Galatia and Phrygia, where he visited the churches founded on the first and second journeys. Traveling through Phrygia, famous for its pasturelands and its wool industry, Paul followed the beautiful road running down the river Meander, whose winding course has enriched the English language with the expression "meandering".

He passed through Colossae—in spite of its imposing name, a small forgotten townlet. In the area around Ephesus were many Christian strongholds, mentioned only later in the Revelation to John, but whose origin probably went back to the times of Paul. An important city was Laodicea, whose pharmaceutical industry was well known, especially for a certain eye-healing salve. According to Cicero one could change money in the bank of Laodicea at a good rate. Hierapolis presents a fantastic appearance with its white terraces of stalactites—deposits of a volcanic spring reaching the temperature of 98 C. These mysterious springs, which could either kill or heal, were sites of worship of numerous Oriental divinities. A deep religiosity appears also in the Stoic Epictetus, a native of this region, as expressed in one of his hymns: "If I were a nightingale, I would sing like a nightingale, if I were a swan I would sing as he does. But I am a man and so can sing only a song of praise to God." In Sardis,

And to the angel of the church in Pergamum write *(Revelation 2:12)*

The Asclepieum of Pergamum, the sanctuary of the Greek god of medicine Asclepius, whose cult was widespread since dim antiquity. The healing art practiced at the Asclepieia was a mixture of the supernatural and the practical.

known for its sizeable Jewish community which had the largest found synagogue, pilgrims' flasks for oil and water have been found, which exhibit some unique decorations illustrating missionary activity: on one side an evangelist sitting on a chair writing a book, on the other a man with a book decorated with a diagonal cross. In Pergamum, though, the situation was different; it was the center of a heathen cult, competing fiercely with the new Church. There, Zeus, whose altar is now in the Berlin museum, and the savior-god Asclepius, were specially revered. This probably earned the place the unsavory name of "Satan's Throne".

EPHESUS AGAIN

Paul now returned to Ephesus, this time for a stay of two and a half years (52–55 AD). The eerily silent and sand-covered site, separated today from the sea by six miles of dunes, was in Paul's time the greatest city of Asia Minor, and one of its biggest harbors. Although Pergamum was the capital, Ephesus was the most important city of the province, and as such the residential site of the proconsuls. Trading with Greece, Sicily, and Spain, Egypt, Syria and the

Black Sea ports by sea, and maintaining a flourishing inland commerce, Ephesus was handling the riches of the East and West.

Ephesus was the center of the worship of Artemis, an Oriental fertility goddess, whose prototype was Astarte, worshiped under different guises throughout the entire Middle East. The cult of the Ephesian Artemis was by no means limited to Ephesus—she was famous all over the Mediterranean, and especially so over the Eastern part of it. Her temple was considered one of the Seven Wonders of the World. An ancient poet, Timotheus described it in these words: "In astonishment I looked on the walls of Babylon, saw the sculpture of Olympian Zeus, admired the hanging gardens in Rhodes and the ruins of the Pyramids and the grave of Mausolus, then I saw the house of Artemis and everything else was as nothing and I said: 'on earth, Helios (the sun-god) himself has never seen anything more beautiful'." The roof of the temple was supported by 127 Ionic columns, its area about two thirds of St. Peter's in Rome. This magnificent temple was completely destroyed by Gothic barbarians in the 3rd century, and its ruins are now buried beneath the

View of Pergamum, one of the great cities of antiquity on the west coast of Asia. It contains one of the most impressive remnants of antiquity—a colossal Roman complex built over the river Selinus which flows across it in a double-vaulted tunnel.

. . . .he has worked hard for you and for those in Laodicea and in Hierapolis *(Colossians 4:13)*

Hierapolis presents a fantastic appearance:
white terraces of solidified sediment of
chemicals deposited by a hot volcanic spring.
Called "Cotton Castle", these petrified
cascades were believed to have burst forth
from the entrance to the nether world.

soil. The cultic image of the goddess, whose breast ornaments, in several rows of egg-shaped decorations, were a sign of eternal fertility, has been preserved in several copies.

Paul was not the first to bring the Word to Ephesus. "Now a Jew, named Apollos, a native of Alexandria, came to Ephesus. He was an eloquent man, well versed in the scripture" (Acts 18:24), as well he might be, coming from Alexandria, one of the greatest cultural centers of antiquity. Though a devout believer, Apollos "knew only the baptism of John" (Acts 18:25) which he taught to the prospective converts. "When Aquila and Priscilla heard him" they, of course "expounded to him the way of God more accurately" (Acts 18:26). Apollos was now in Corinth, but Paul met his disciples, twelve in all, and found that they "have never even heard that there is a Holy Spirit" (Acts 19:2). Then Paul baptized them in the name of the Lord.

The sizeable Jewish community enjoyed certain privileges, such as exemption from military service, unhindered dispatch of funds to Jerusalem, as well as appointments as official municipal physicians.

For three months Paul preached in the synagogue undisturbed, and his success must have been considerable, since, as usual, it produced opposition. He then did an unprecedented thing: leaving the synagogue, he withdrew with his disciples into a hall rented from one Tyrannus, probably a teacher of Greek rhetoric. There Paul taught daily for two years.

Extensive excavations have facilitated the restoration of old Ephesus. From the harbor a thirty-five feet wide marble-paved and pillar-lined street led into the interior of the city. Paul would have approached the city through this street, entering it through the northern gate, called the Magnesian. According to the ancient law of architectural aesthetics, a street could not lose itself in a distant void; a glance along it required a harmonious end on which it could rest. So in compliance with architectural harmony, the great harbor street culminated in a marvelous edifice—the theater.

A stroll through the excavations would lead us through places of interest as variegated as human inventiveness could make them. We come upon ruins of a large brothel: frequenting such establishments in pagan antiquity bore no social stigma. Nearby a

The top of an ancient Jewish sarcophagus decorated with an engraved *menorah* and a high relief of a lion's head, found on the site of ancient Hierapolis, testifies to the presence of a Jewish community to which Paul would address himself as was his custom.

'Great is Artemis of the Ephesians!' (Acts 19:28)

Artemis of the Ephesians (left), the goddess whose temple supported by a hundred columns was one of the "Seven Wonders of the World". The great theater of Ephesus (right), the scene of the uproar caused by the silversmiths in defense of their goddess Artemis.

gaming board was found bearing the inscription: "the board that gives you pleasure through loss of money"—a clever allusion to the pleasures of gambling which are not affected by losing. Opposite the brothel we come upon the library of Celsus, whose reading room was built on arched substructures to keep the moisture out. Scrolls of manuscripts were kept in closed-like niches, arranged in three rows, one above the other. Among the scrolls would, no doubt, have been the works of Homer and Heraclitus, written in that city. The Orient invented the alphabet, loved the written word, and was thus a land of the book. The builder of the library willed himself to be buried therein, in order to be surrounded forever by his beloved books.

Thus archaeology provides the background for a better understanding of Paul's exhortations, in which prostitution, drunkenness and dishonesty figured prominently. In particular he attacked idleness in which he saw one of the main social evils. He called time and again for perseverance in obedience to the head of the household, since life is based on the principle of order, in the center of which is the Lord.

'Awake, O sleeper, and arise from the dead, and Christ shall give you light' *(Ephesians 5:14)*

The Grotto of the Seven Sleepers of Ephesus (left). To escape the obligation to perform a pagan sacrifice, these young Christians left the city and fell asleep in a cave. The facade of emperor Hadrian's temple (right) which earned Ephesus the coveted title of Neocorus—"Temple Warden".

THE GRAND BONFIRE OF MAGIC

Trashy literature abounded as well, on diverse subjects, as in our own day. But the most popular and flourishing were manuals of magic. Ephesus specialized in a magical prescription, known as "Ephesia grammata". These charms could be used as love potions and talismans for all occasions and were therefore in great demand. These superstitions became useful, though unsolicited, allies in Paul's work. Belief in the occult powers of Jewish exorcists was widespread (Elymas in Cyprus, Acts 13:8–11, for instance).

Paul's personal charisma had become famous, to such an extent, that the clothes which had been in contact with his body "were carried away" (Acts 19:11) to cure the sick. To some "professional miracle-makers" Paul's success was a good business indeed. There was in Ephesus a Jew named Sceva, who, together with his seven sons, had a prosperous thaumaturgic "business". They decided to try Paul's methods of healing, a case which took a rather unexpected and comic turn. They approached a man possessed of an evil spirit and exorcised him with these words: "I adjure you by the Jesus whom Paul

preaches." Whereupon the man (or the evil spirit) answered scornfully: "Jesus I know, and Paul I know; but who are you?" Then he leapt upon the would-be exorcists and gave them a thorough thrashing, "so that they fled out of that house naked and wounded" (Acts 19:13–16).

Paul's reputation was now supreme, but he refuted vigorously all notion of magic—his power was in his faith. This brought a chain-reaction—many believers confessed to dabbling in magic arts; who in Ephesus did not to a greater or lesser extent? Others followed, even professed magicians. The result was a huge, free-for-all bonfire. Talismans, charms, amulets, collections of magical formulae and manuals on magic all went up in flames—the writings alone valued at the impressive sum of 50,000 "pieces of silver" (about $3,000). Making the Ephesians divest themselves of their magic charms, aside from the cost of it, Paul could have safely considered half the challenge met!

During those years in Ephesus Paul maintained a severe daily schedule; in the early morning hours he sat at his loom, faithful as ever to the tenet that a man ought to work for his living. Not in vain had the rabbinical sages admonished that the "... study (Torah) which is not combined with work falls into neglect in the end, and becomes the cause of sin" (Abot. 2:2). In the early afternoon hours he taught his disciples and preached to all comers in the hall of Tyrannus. He received visitors from all over the province. He also found time to write to his "children", in Galatia, Philippi and Corinth. His church in Ephesus grew and prospered. Paul had every reason to be satisfied with the results of his work in Ephesus, and so he began to consider that from then on his work there could be carried on by his disciples. He was becoming restless again. His intention was now to revisit his churches in Macedonia and Achaia, then to go to Jerusalem and finally, he felt "he must also see Rome" (Acts 19:21). Having laid his plans carefully, he sent ahead to Greece his helpers, Timothy and Erastus. For once, he could have expected an orderly and friendly departure from a city where he was so successful and felt so secure. But it was not given him: his plans were rudely upset by a sudden, but not totally surprising outburst of rioting.

"GREAT IS ARTEMIS OF THE EPHESIANS!" There was in Ephesus a man named Demetrius, probably a senior member of the guild of silversmiths. This Demetrius called the other members together and reminded them that they earned their living by making little replicas of the shrine of Artemis, for pilgrims to take home as souvenirs of their visit. "And you see and hear that not only in Ephesus but almost throughout all Asia this Paul has persuaded and turned away a considerable company of people, saying that gods made with hands are not gods. And there is danger not only that this trade of ours may come into disrepute but also the temple of the great goddess Artemis may count for nothing, and that she may even be deposed from her magnificence, she whom all Asia and the world worship" (Acts 19:26–27). Using such convincing arguments as loss of livelihood, touching upon feelings of pride in, and religious attachment to, their goddess could not but produce the expected reaction. The silversmiths thus incited and incensed rushed out into the streets, a most effective rallying cry on their lips: "Great is Artemis of the Ephesians!" In no time they filled the city with confusion. Unable to find Paul they dragged his Macedonian travel companions Gaius and Aristarchus with them, and followed by a great mob they all converged upon the theater, as the most convenient place for an assembly. Hearing what had happened, Paul wished to go there immediately, but was prevented by his friends. To venture among a riotous crowd and attempt to address them when everybody was shouting at the same time "and most... did not know why they had come together" (Acts 19:32), was sheer madness. Jews and Christians were often lumped together in cases like that, therefore a Jew named Alexander attempted to address the assembly, in order to prove that his community was in no way involved in the silversmiths' grievances. But having recognized him as a Jew, the mob hooted him down and continued to work itself up into towering hysterics, keeping up an incessant chant "Great is Artemis of the Ephesians" for two long hours. Judging correctly that the mob would by now be much more amenable to reason, having spent their rage in two hours of howling, the town clerk calmed them down. He pointed out that the city of the Ephesians was temple-keeper of the great

147

. . . the next day we touched at Samos *(Acts 20:15)*

Samos, the island which was the mirror of Ionian perfection in shipbuilding, architecture and engineering. Paul's stop on the island was short—they stayed only overnight. The huge columns (right), are the remnants of the great temple of Zeus' consort, Hera, on Samos.

Artemis—an established and unquestionable fact known to all; that the two men were neither sacrilegious nor blasphemers of their goddess. Thus there was no need to do anything rash. "If Demetrius and the craftsmen with him have a complaint against any one, the courts are open, and there are proconsuls; let them bring charges . . ." (Acts 19:38). And here he served them a neat reminder: "For we are in danger of being charged with rioting today, there being no cause that we can give to justify this commotion" (Acts 19:40). This had a most sobering effect. He bid the crowd to disperse, which it did without further ado.

This rather farcical episode had a very serious background. For Paul it was a sign of a growing opposition, headed primarily by simple folk worried about their livelihood. In reality, despite certain successes, a deep shadow lay over Ephesus: "I am in peril every hour. I fought with beasts at Ephesus" (I Cor. 15:32). Clouds were brewing against him from all sides. His opponents had begun hunting him down. He received bad news also from other communities, especially Galatia and Corinth, where on one visit a hot-head had gravely insulted him, so that on his return he was to write: "I wrote you out of much affliction and anguish of heart and with many tears, not to cause you pain, but to let you know the abundant love that I have for you" (II Cor. 2:4). In Ephesus he was arrested and put in the custody of the praetorian guard. Though the imprisonment was light—he was allowed to receive visitors and write letters—there was no knowing how the trial would end, nor do we know the immediate cause of his arrest.

On top of one of the hills rises an impressive tower of a fortress which, since some unrecorded period, has been considered the site of Paul's imprisonment; through the wide, open gaps of the tower whistles the wind. Who is this Paul? We look at the ruins of the great city, but no answer comes from them. We look at the Byzantine church which contains the grave of the evangelist John, active in Ephesus a generation later: from this church too, no echo comes forth. One looks in vain in the book of John's "Revelation" for Paul's name. To the northeast lies a large graveyard about which the legend of the "Seven Sleepers" is woven. The vast necropolis, a sign of once flourishing Christian life, is now a

and the day after that we came to Miletus *(Acts 20:15)*

Storks in the ruins of Miletus, the great maritime city
of the archaic period, mistress of the Aegean and birthplace
of science and philosophy.

And from Miletus he sent to Ephesus and called to him the elders of the church (Acts 20:17)

Ruins of the theater of Miletus (below).
The Baths of Faustina (left)
are of the usual Roman style. In the
frigidarium (cold room) is the reclining
statue of the river-god Meander.

meeting-place of jackals who bid "good night" to each other. And in the east, in the middle of a grandiose mountain landscape, have come to light the foundations of a house from the 1st century, in which allegedly Mary lived. A chapel was built on the site, the only Christian sanctuary in the region. It nevertheless symbolizes Paul, who despite all his failures never despaired, but pursued his goal with unequaled zeal, as in the refrain of an old liturgical hymn: "Awake, O sleeper, and arise from the dead, and Christ shall give you light" (Eph. 5:14).

Paul was released from prison but since attempts were made on his life he left the city never to return.

FAREWELL TO HELLAS

Back at Corinth Paul had reason to rejoice: he found the community at peace. There he also made his plans for what was to be his last visit to Jerusalem. His immediate purpose was to take thither a collection for the poor brethren. "For Macedonia and Achaia have been pleased to make some contribution for the poor among the saints at Jerusalem" (Rom. 15:26). From Jerusalem he intended to go to Rome. This "Jerusalem and Rome axis", of his spiritual capital and the capital of the political world, must have been in his mind already for some time as an essential basis on which to build his universal church (Perowne).

Here in Corinth he wrote his famous letter to the Romans (ca. 58 AD) in which he announced his coming visit "passing as I go to Spain" (Rom. 15:24). But before undertaking it he was bound for Jerusalem. He asked the community to join him in prayer for the success of his mission: the safe delivery of alms contributed by Christian brethren for the saints of Jerusalem. He regarded these alms not only as material support for the Jerusalem community, but mainly as a sign of unity between Jewish and Gentile Christians, which was threatened by his opponents.

On his return trip he had to change his route for fear of ambushes. Therefore instead of going by sea, as was his original intent, he went by a land route, sending his companions ahead by another route to an agreed meeting point. However dangerous the situation, Paul would not be diverted from the immediate goal he had set for himself: the voyage to Jerusalem. Nor would the entreaties of the brethren have any effect upon his set decision.

Passing again through Macedonia, he celebrated Passover at Philippi. Then he crossed from Neapolis to Troas, where he joined the representatives of the churches who were to go with him, carrying the collection for the needy brethren in Jerusalem. Luke relates to us a curious episode in Troas: "On the first day of the week"—it was already the custom of the Christians to meet at prayer on the day of the Resurrection (our Sunday)—they "were gathered to break bread." This "first day" was all the more significant, since they were "intending to leave on the morrow." Paul preached "and he prolonged his speech until midnight." The meeting was held in an upper room on the third storey. The heat generating from the "many lights in the upper chamber where (they) were gathered" and the large assembly of people as well as Paul's interminable discourse made one young man named Eutychus, who was sitting on the ledge of a window, drowsy. He fell asleep and toppled over onto the paved street. When he was taken up for dead, the assembly was dismayed but not so Paul. Coolly, in perfect control of the situation, Paul bent over the lad, embraced him and proclaimed him alive. Then he went on with the bread-breaking and resumed his sermon till the small hours of the morning. From the point of view of humor Paul's oratorical talents may be doubtful—but his presence of mind, his absolute command of a situation no matter how distressing, fills us with wonder.

HUES OF THE MOST MARVELOUS BLUE

The following morning Paul's companions set sail for Assos, the most beautiful Greek city in Asia and Europe. Its magnificent rock-hewn citadel, the two-mile long walls and battlements are still there to meet the curious traveler's eye. Paul reached Assos by a land route. There they boarded the ship to begin Paul's last voyage to Jerusalem. Traveling through the Aegean, between the coast and the island, amid the hues of most marvelous blue—sky, sea and the mountains of the mainland—has always been an experience of unequaled beauty.

First came Mytilene, then the great harbor of Lesbos, the island made famous by the immortal poetess, Sapho. Then came the beautiful island of Chios, Homer's alleged birthplace, the site of the

. . . we came by a straight course to Cos, and the next day to Rhodes, . . . (Acts 21:1)

The Asclepieum of Cos (below), the island which was the home of Hippocrates, the 5th century B.C. Greek doctor honored as the father of medicine, whose name is immortalized by the oath taken by all physicians the world over. An imposing colonnade of the temple of Athena Lindia, the greek goddess of wisdom, graces the acropolis of Lindos (right), the main city of Rhodes.

great shrine of the goddess Cybele. Sailing past Ephesus, the following day they entered Samos, famous for its temple to Hera, Zeus' consort. But its abiding pride was its illustrious son, Pythagoras.

The following day they reached Miletus. The beautiful harbor city had the master-builder, Hippodamus, to thank for its famous architectural planning, which was to serve as a model for many other cities. Its remarkable harbor, like so many others, is now silted up. There is evidence of a large Jewish community, in the form of a letter from the Roman governor to the municipal authorities, granting the Jews freedom of religious worship, this privilege being disputed by the local authorities. In the well-preserved theater, there were reserved seats for the "God-fearers", an interesting example of the broad-mindedness of the Diaspora Jews, for whom regular attendance at the theater was a requirement of general culture. Miletus was the scene of Paul's parting from a community he was particularly attached to, the Ephesians. Had he not spent more time in their midst than anywhere else? Sailing past Ephesus some days earlier, Paul had recoiled from the idea of stopping at the city, where the pastoral happiness he had enjoyed there and his departure were marred by his imprisonment. Thus he sent some of his companions to Ephesus, 30 miles up the Meander, to summon the elders of the city to Miletus, in order to greet and take leave of them.

When they arrived, Paul delivered his valediction. It was a farewell, for Paul knew that he was never to see them again. He reminded them to follow his example, to work not for material gain, but to support themselves and those who were in need. "In all things I have shown you that by so toiling one must help the weak, remembering the words of the Lord Jesus . . . 'It is more blessed to give than to receive'" (Acts 20:35). He himself was "going to Jerusalem bound in the spirit, not knowing what shall befall me there except that imprisonment and afflictions await me" (Acts 20:22). The very essence of his life is contained in these words of his: "But I do not account my life of any value, nor as precious to myself, if only I may accomplish my course and the ministry which I received from the Lord Jesus, to testify to the Gospel of the grace of God" (Acts 20:24). When he finished they were overcome by grief, "they all wept and embraced Paul and kissed him, sorrowing most . . . that they should see his face no more" (Acts 20:37).

They accompanied him to the coaster. Since his thoughts were carrying him to Jerusalem, he scarcely took notice of the places his ship was bearing him past. The coaster made for the charming island of Cos, home of Hippocrates, the father of medicine, with its sanctuaries and sanatoria devoted to the healing god, Asclepius. According to a local tradition, he remained somewhat longer on Rhodes. There he would have landed in the bay of Lindos, over which towered the acropolis with its famous temple to Athena Lindia, built over a sacred grotto.

The final port of call of the coaster was Patara in Lycia. Today it is a sleepy, forlorn townlet, but in Paul's time its temple of Apollo rivaled the one in Delphi in fame and prestige, and as a haven and sanctuary too. In Patara, the travelers left the coaster and boarded a ship crossing to Phoenicia. Sailing southeast and passing within sight of the west end of Cyprus, they came down to Phoenicia at Tyre, where the ship was to discharge its cargo.

On his earlier voyages Paul must have passed through Phoenicia, since there is a tradition related to his presence in a small bay north of Beirut.

TYRE—THE PRINCE OF MERCHANTS

Tyre had since the dawn of history been one of the greatest trade centers of the Orient, one of the two chief cities of the Phoenicians, the unsurpassed traders and mariners of antiquity. The riches and opulence of Tyre and Sidon testified to the scope of commerce commanded by them. The excavations of ancient Tyre, among which municipal buildings as well as magnificent tombs stand out, convey an impressive picture from Paul's time. The city had the right to strike its own coins; Tyre's money was the hard currency of antiquity, accepted in payment everywhere. Even the Temple tax had to be paid in "Phoenician dollars". The Phoenician merchant ships were incomparable. Vestiges of their presence were found as far away as Granada, and they may have sailed as far as England and southern Scandinavia. The early Viking vessels bear a striking resemblance to the sturdy Phoenician men-of-war. When King Solomon was about to build his famous temple in Jerusalem, it was to King Hiram of Tyre

. . . and landed at Tyre; for there the ship was to unload its cargo

(Acts 21:3)

In ancient times purple garments were the prerogative of kings and rulers. Since remote antiquity Phoenicia was the "land of the purple" as its coasts abounded in the shellfish represented here, from which the priceless color was extracted and then exported from Phoenicia's main ports Tyre and Sidon.

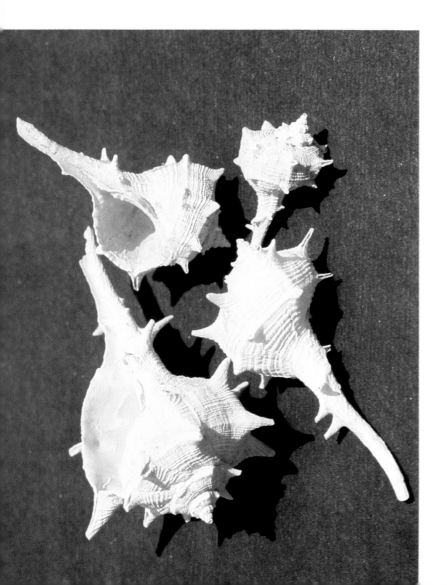

that he applied to have wood from the "cedars of Lebanon" cut for him. Four centuries later, Ezekiel was to give a majestic description of Tyre's riches—"your builders made perfect your beauty" (Ez. 27:4), and "every precious stone was your covering" (Ez. 28:13).

The far-reaching Phoenician merchantmen carried every imaginable ware—wool and wine, fruits and cattle, horses, slaves, metals (iron, copper and gold), precious stones from East Africa and India, spices and textiles, monkeys and exotic birds, ivory tusks and ebony. Especially famous was their own product, the Tyrian dye, of which the finest purple cloth, so highly prized in antiquity, was made.

The most imperishable ware they carried and were unwittingly to bequeath to mankind as a priceless gift was the alphabet. The ancient Semitic script, which evolved into the Hebrew we know today was adapted by the Phoenicians and carried by them through the then known world, to emerge finally as the alphabet—the "aleph" and "beth" in Hebrew, the "a" and "b" in Latin and Cyrillic scripts. But splendid Tyre was doomed to perish, to become "a place for the spreading of nets" (Ez. 26:5).

6. FAREWELL JERUSALEM

In Tyre Paul heard the depressing news from Judaea. Paul's opponents from Asia Minor, now on pilgrimage in Judaea, were joining forces with those in Jerusalem. The Roman procurator, Ventidius Cumanus (48–52 AD), conducted his office in a manner that was nothing short of insulting. His mercenaries were pagans from Samaria and Caesarea—on notoriously bad terms with the Jews. This precipitated the inevitable. Indecent behavior of a soldier in the Temple precincts brought on a riot; Samaritans attacked passing Galileans; the Jews retaliated, and a bloody free-for-all began. The Samaritans appealed to the governor of Syria, Ummidius Quadratus, who was at that time in Tyre, accusing the Jews of setting their villages on fire and plundering them. The Jews countered that the Samaritans were the originators of the violence that now spread over Judaea. They claimed that Cumanus had been corrupted by the Samaritans' gifts not to prosecute those guilty of murder. Several Jews were crucified and the matter was transferred to Rome.

But the situation was in no way improved by the appointment of Antonius Felix to the procuratorship. Felix was a freedman of Claudius' mother, Antonia, whence his name. When he set out to suppress the unrest, he did it with more than the usual measure of Roman cruelty. Daylight assault was followed by night assassinations and the reign of terror began. Villages were terrorized, towns were unsafe, roads at the mercy of robbers. And it was the procurator himself, the very man whose foremost duty it was to maintain order and administer justice, who provoked the violence, as if to illustrate the well-known Hebrew saying—"a slave become king."

For Paul the situation was especially dangerous, since the "Hellenists" favored the Samaritans, as we have seen above.

"THE WILL OF THE LORD BE DONE"

During the seven days of Paul's stay in Tyre, the brethren there pleaded with him not to proceed to Jerusalem; but to no avail. In spite of his forebodings "that imprisonment and afflictions" awaited him there, he took leave of the Tyrian disciples who accompanied him to the shore praying there for his welfare.

From Tyre they sailed down the coast to Ptole-

161

The biblical Akko, originally a Phoecician town, was renamed Ptolemais in the 4th century B.C. after Ptolemy II of Egypt. Only after the Arab conquest in the 7th century A.D. it reverted to its original name Akko. The city Ptolemais-Akko, built on a rocky promontory at the northern end of the Haifa bay, was the Mediterranean port of Galilee. Here Paul greeted the brethren on his last return journey to Jerusalem.

mais, at the northern end of the Carmel range. The charming little town was called Akko in Biblical times and was renamed Ptolemais in the 4th century BC after one of Alexander's generals, Ptolemy. It reverted to its original Semitic name Akko after the Arab conquest in the 7th century. The Crusaders converted it into a formidable fortress and changed its original name Akko into St. Jean d'Acre, the name of the Knights of St. John.

Paul stayed in Ptolemais one day only—to greet the brethren—and sailed south to Caesarea. In this magnificent port city, one of the masterpieces of Herod's architectural skill, with its predominant Roman-Gentile population, Paul and his companions felt at ease. They stayed in the house of Philip, one of the seven evangelists. As in Tyre, here too the brethren implored Paul not to venture into Jerusalem. The plea was most dramatically presented to him by Agabus, the prophet who had arrived from Judaea and knew exactly what Paul could expect there. Like Jeremiah of old, who to illustrate the impending subjugation of Jerusalem had donned yoke-bars on his shoulders and thus appeared in the streets of Jerusalem, so Agabus now took Paul's

Fishing was Akko's main source of income. The Crusaders converted the town into their main harbor in the 12th century renaming it St. Jean d'Acre. The heavy battlements and walls (right) date mainly from the 18th century and are of Turkish workmanship.

When we had finished the voyage from Tyre, we arrived at Ptolemais; and we greeted the brethren . . . (Acts 21:7)

On the morrow we departed and came to Caesarea *(Acts 21:8)*

Mole of Herod's harbor in Caesarea (left), the magnificent city of Herod the Great founded in the year 22 B.C. and named after Herod's friend and benefactor Caesar Augustus. Below, exquisite glassware found in a Roman villa in Caesarea.

girdle and bound his own feet and hands saying that thus would Paul be bound in Jerusalem. But Paul was adamant. "What are you doing weeping and breaking my heart? For I am ready not only to be imprisoned but even to die at Jerusalem for the name of Lord Jesus" (Acts 21:13).

PERSONA NON GRATA

The party accompanied by some disciples from Caesarea then set out for Jerusalem. Paul chose to lodge in the house of Mnason, an early and trusted disciple, on the outskirts of the city. It was obvious that the incendiary mood prevailing at that moment in Jerusalem made Paul "persona non grata", to say the least: to the Judeo-Christians he was a Hellenizer who disregarded the Law; to the orthodox Jews he was anathema, and for the Romans an irritant—yet another cause of rioting.

It was Shavuot 58 AD, the harvest festival which expresses the connection between the people of Israel and their land, and commemorates the revelation at Sinai: the giving of the Law, where the Jewish people received the basis for their special identity. It was one of the three biblical pilgrimage festivals for which Jews streamed from the Diaspora to the Holy City. This was the immediate setting against which we must view the internal and external tensions to which Paul now saw himself exposed. An inner religiosity and tradition were drawing him to Jerusalem, but "his" Jerusalem—in the form of the numerous Jewish Christians, who precisely at this time were being reminded of the significance of the Law—was by no means eager to have him there then.

The atmosphere was friendly at the first meeting with James and the elders, but nevertheless marked with constraint. After greeting the brethren, Paul related in detail the results of his ministry among the Gentiles and the grace that was done to him by allowing him to bring many heathen into the Faith. In that the brethren rejoiced, but what of the painful question that "you teach all the Jews who are among the Gentiles to forsake Moses, telling them not to circumcise their children or observe the customs?" (Acts 21:21). The problem had, of course, at one point been settled in principle, on the occasion of the gathering of the apostles. But in Jerusalem the question was not very relevant, since

Jewish-Christians did not live with Gentile-Christians to any real extent. What was then to be done with the collection he carried? It would not be accepted since it came from heretics. Anyone familiar with Oriental customs of hospitality and reciprocal gift-giving, deeply ingrained to this day as an integral part of Oriental social life, will realize what an affront for Paul this rejection would have been, the spurning of the collection he had taken up with such love. It might have led to a final breach between him and the Jerusalem church. But the venerable, quiet James, who now headed the community, advised him to conform to the usages expected of a guest: he should undergo the seven-day purification, prescribed for all Jews returning from foreign parts, and participate in a ceremony of discharging the vows of four poor Nazarites, paying their expenses for the prescribed sacrifices. This would vindicate Paul publicly as a Jew who observed the Law and performed an act of charity—an important commandment in the Jewish law. Moreover the compliance with James' suggestion conformed to his own principle: "To the Jews I became as a Jew; . . . To those outside the law I became as one out-side the law . . . under the law of Christ" (I Cor. 9:20–21). This event is illustrated by two ossuaries carrying the inscription "Hanania, son of Jonathan the Nazarite". Found on the Mount of Olives, they are the only known instances of evidence of the Nazarite vow.

AN EXERCISE IN FUTILITY

Soon afterwards events moved rapidly. While in the Temple on the seventh day, the day of release from the vow, Paul was recognized by some Jews from Ephesus, who were particularly incensed at seeing him there during the holiday week: "This is the man who is teaching men everywhere against the people and the law and this place" (Acts 21:28). In their emotional outburst they put forward as fact the accusation of what had not and could never happen, unless Paul were a villain or a fool: the accusation that he had brought heathens into the inner ante-court of the Temple. In order to understand the gravity of the accusation, we must remember that the Temple of Jerusalem consisted of various parts, with different regulations governing admission to each of them. The Holy of Holies could be entered

My manner of life from my youth, spent from the beginning among my own nation and at Jerusalem . . . (Acts 26:4)

A bird's-eye view of present-day Jerusalem, that ancient city so beloved of Paul.

only by the High Priest, and even by him only once a year, on the Day of Atonement. The Temple proper and the court in front of it, except the altar, could be approached only by the priests. Male Israelites could enter the Inner Court; women could only go as far as the Women's Court, the outer of the two courts of the Inner Temple. Gentiles were free to enter the Temple esplanade up to the low barrier encircling the Inner Temple (we have evidence of pilgrimages made by Gentiles coming to offer sacrifices to God), but might not pass beyond. Infringement of these regulations was punished by death by the Roman authorities, and the mere suspicion of an illicit entry by a Gentile beyond the permitted limits would arouse the wrath of the populace. In order to prevent such incidents, inscriptions were set up beside the barrier of the Inner Temple, warning non-Jews against trespassing, on pain of death.

Therefore such an insensate act would be the last thing to cross Paul's mind. What brought the suspicion on him was his close association with Gentiles in general. Moreover, he had been seen walking through the city with Trophimus, a Gentile from

171

When I had returned to Jerusalem and was praying in the temple, . . . and saw him saying to me . . . (Acts 22:17)

The Temple Mount today—the site where Solomon's First Temple had stood, and where after its destruction the Second Temple was erected. Here Paul came to be released from his vow. The Dome of the Rock, a Moslem shrine, stands near the site of the ancient temple of the Jews.

Ephesus. The outcry provoked a riot, something the Romans had been at pains to avoid at all costs. The Temple gates were closed in the face of the spreading uproar and Paul was pushed down into the narrow streets of the Tyropoeon valley. Some saw this as a favorable opportunity to kill Paul there and then, which would undoubtedly have happened but for a Roman sentry on guard duty in the Temple who "sent a word to the tribune of the cohorts that all Jerusalem was in confusion" (Acts 21:31). The tribune and his centurions ran down to them and practically tore Paul out of the mob's hands. Paul was then arrested and bound in chains. But when the tribune sought to discover who he was and what he had done to cause such an outburst, he could learn nothing from the contradictory shouts of the crowd. The confusion was such that to bring Paul into the barracks the Romans actually had to carry him out of reach of the incensed crowds.

It was a narrow escape indeed, but Paul was by now used to being the most hated man in the city and thus the object of mob violence. Therefore, before being carried into the fortress, with perfect composure and calm he turned and addressed the tribune, astonishing the Roman by his perfect Greek. Paul introduced himself: "I am a Jew from Tarsus in Cilicia, a citizen of no mean city; I beg you, let me speak to the people." To try to do that was an exercise in futility—Paul must have realized that. He was ready to die for his faith—but to be accused of acts which he as a Jew would never have committed was breaking his heart. He felt a profound need to clear himself before his people. The Roman, impressed by Paul's bearing and composure, gave him leave to speak and Paul's soul went out to his people in these words: "Brethren and fathers, hear the defense which I now make before you" (Acts 22:1). Standing on the steps leading to the fortress Antonia, Paul addressed them in Hebrew. Hearing the "heretic" addressing them in the refined Hebrew of a rabbinical scholar had an electrifying effect on the multitude. Minutes before, they had clamored for his death. Now a hushed silence fell upon them. Paul then brought forth the justification of his life and conduct: ". . . a Jew born in Tarsus, brought up in this city at the feet of Gamaliel . . . educated according to the strict manner of the Law of our fathers . . . zealous for God" (Acts 22:3). He re-

. . .for he was hastening to be at Jerusalem, if possible, on the day of Pentecost (Acts 20:16)

One of the three pilgrim festivals, the Feast of Weeks (Pentecost) celebrated today at the Western Wall. During Passover, Pentecost and the Feast of Tabernacles the "congregation of Israel" thronged to the Temple to celebrate the festivals, and Paul too would be among the worshippers.

counted in detail his journey to Damascus, especially the event at the gates of that city. Then came the conversion, return to Jerusalem, the dream in the Temple with God's order to leave Jerusalem and His commission to go among the Gentiles. . . .

But having been away for so many years, Paul was unaware of the extent of the resentment that had built up against the *Gentiles*, whom the Jews identified with their heathen oppressors—the Romans, and the suffering and indignity inflicted upon them by the latter. Thus at the very mention of the word "Gentiles", the riot broke out in all fury, accompanied by renewed demands for Paul's death: "Away with such a fellow from the earth!" (Acts 22:22). "Earth" is to be meant as "land", the separation of Paul as "unclean", from the Land of Israel. It came as a shock to him, who was so closely attached to his homeland. In this connection we can understand the consolation extended to him by the Lord the following night: "Take courage! For as you have testified about me at Jerusalem, so you must bear witness also at Rome" (Acts 23:11).

TO SCOURGE A ROMAN CITIZEN?

The Roman officer, unable to make anything out of this confusing scene, and conscious only of his responsibility of keeping the city quiet, ordered Paul, in his crude Roman fashion, "to be examined by scourging", a means of investigation used in cases where non-Romans and slaves were involved. Faced with the indignity and torture of scourging, Paul then raised the issue of his Roman citizenship and the rights it accorded him. One can almost imagine Paul relishing the effect his cool, ironic question: "Is it lawful for you to scourge a man that is a Roman, and uncondemned?" (Acts 22:25) must have had upon the bewildered centurion. To scourge a Roman citizen? The words produced the desired effect. The centurion ran to the tribune, the full meaning of his alarm at such an offence contained in the question he threw at him: "What are you about to do?" The tribune came at once. "Tell me, are you a Roman citizen?" When Paul confirmed it, the incredulous Roman remarked: "I bought this citizenship for a large sum." "But I was born a citizen", came Paul's unruffled reply. That was more than enough for the poor tribune. The "examina-

. . . Paul, standing on the steps, . . . spoke to them in the Hebrew language, saying: 'Brethren and fathers, hear the defence which I now make before you' (Acts 21:40, 22:1)

The Temple of Jerusalem consisted of several courts the entrance to which was subject to strict regulations: each was separated by a barrier carrying inscriptions in Greek (below) and Hebrew warning against trespassing. The reconstructed model of the Antonia fortress (right), where Paul standing on the steps addressed the crowd assembled on the temple esplanade, bringing forth the *apologia pro vita sua*—the justification of his life and conduct.

...he (the tribune) ordered him to be brought into the barracks

(Acts 21:34)

The site on which the fortress Antonia, built by Herod the Great and named by him after his friend Mark Antony, stood guarding the northwest corner of the temple esplanade. Seen beyond the trees are the rock-cuttings which are the only vestiges of the ancient fortress. On top of these are Moslem buildings of Mameluke construction.

tion" was hastily canceled and the officer was left asking himself how he was to face the eventual question of why he had bound a Roman citizen.

"BRETHREN, I AM A PHARISEE"

Hoping the Jews would have calmed down during the night, the tribune summoned the Sanhedrin, and the following morning brought Paul before them. The meeting started off badly with a heated exchange between Paul and the presiding elder, a former high priest named Ananias, a totally unscrupulous man. The Sanhedrin was composed of Sadducees and Pharisees, therefore Paul came out with a ringing appeal to his party: "Brethren, I am a Pharisee, a son of Pharisees; with respect to the hope and the resurrection of the dead I am on trial".

The Sadducees, selected from the more well-to-do and distinguished ranks of society, were strictly attached to the observance of the Mosaic law in its literal sense. They rejected the immortality of the soul as a concept that received no countenance from the divine book. By virtue of their social rank, they monopolized the high priesthood. To the authority of the Scriptures, the Pharisees, on the other hand,

added that of tradition and the interpretation of the Law—the Oral Law. Within its scope came additional articles of faith, such as predestination, future rewards or punishments, the immortality of the soul and the resurrection of the dead. The Pharisees by the austerity of their manners had drawn into their party the main body of the Jewish people.

Thus on points of theology, Paul knew he could expect support from the Pharisees, since "the Sadducees say that there is no resurrection, nor angel, nor spirit; but the Pharisees acknowledge them all" (Acts 23:8). Paul's appeal to the Pharisees can best be understood in the light of what is admirably stated by Prof. William Foxwell Albright: "Yet we may whole-heartedly accept the rehabilitation of the Pharisees, who were God-fearing men with views which closely approximated standard Christian theological positions with respect to the attributes of God, the question of predestination and free will, and the problem of after-life" (From Stone Age to Christianity, pp. 390–391).

As anticipated by Paul, "some of the scribes of the Pharisee party stood up and contended 'We find nothing wrong in this man'" (Acts 23:9). This

178

So the soldiers, . . . took Paul and brought him by night to Antipatris (Acts 23:31)

Antipatris, where Paul and his escort stopped
overnight on their way to Caesarea. On the site of
the biblical Aphek, Herod had built a city which
he named in honor of his father Antipater.
The big mound is crowned by the ruins of a
medieval Crusader castle.

caused an uproar. The assembly was divided and a
loud and violent argument broke out. But Lysias,
the tribune, was not interested in Jewish theology
and did not feel inclined to see the outcome of the
argument. There was already trouble enough with
this Roman citizen, without risking now having him
torn to pieces by the dissenting parties. He "commanded the soldiers to go down" (the Sanhedrin
met within the Temple precincts) "and take him by
force from them." Paul must have been thoroughly
annoyed at this "forced" rescue, since that forum
represented for him an excellent opportunity to state
his case before the Sanhedrin, with numerous sup-
porters from among the Pharisees present. But Lysias had had enough. He would take no risks, and
so he kept him safe in the Antonia fortress.

ESCORT FIT FOR A KING
But for some of the fanatics, Paul was not only an
adversary holding different views on points of theology, but an enemy—and precisely because of his
supreme erudition and powerful intellect, a dangerous one. Therefore a group of 40 fanatics bound
themselves by an oath to abstain from food and

181

*Then he (the tribune) called two o[f]
two hundred soldiers . . . (Acts 23:23[)]*

When Paul was sent under guard to Caesarea
he was accompanied by an unusually strong
detachment of soldiers. This statuette shows
a Roman soldier in standard gear. His
arms—a short sword, a spear and a shield
are missing here.

drink until they had killed Paul. They suggested
that the Sanhedrin request Lysias to send Paul to
appear before the court again with the idea that
they would lay an ambush and kill Paul on the way.
This however reached the ears of Paul's nephew,
who, without wasting a moment, ran to the fortress
and warned his uncle. Paul then called one of the
centurions and asked him to bring the lad to the
tribune, since he had a message for him. The tribune
received him kindly and taking him aside asked
what was it the young man wanted to tell him.
Paul's nephew explained the plot, adding that now
the conspirators were only waiting for Lysias' tacit
agreement. Dismissing the young man, Lysias
bound him to secrecy. This, Claudius Lysias felt,
was really too much. He immediately ordered a
heavy guard, consisting of "two hundred soldiers
with seventy horsemen and two hundred spearmen"
to set out three hours after sunset, escorting Paul
to Caesarea, with express orders to "bring him safely to Felix the governor" (Acts 23:23). Lysias was
taking no more risks with this Roman citizen, and
there was more than enough trouble in Jerusalem
without his causing more.

He wrote an explanatory letter to the governor, to be remitted to Felix personally by the officer in charge of the detachment. In this communication he gave an outline of the case—how he had rescued Paul from the hands of the populace having learnt that he was a Roman citizen. As far as he could make out Paul "was accused about questions of their law, but charged with nothing deserving death or imprisonment" (Acts 23:29). Since he discovered a plot to kill this man he decided to send him to the governor, and ordered his accusers to state their case before Felix. Thus Paul left Jerusalem, which he was never to see again.

The soldiers brought Paul by night to Antipatris, the fortress Herod had named after his father, Antipater. It stood by the sources of the Yarkon river at a highly important strategic position, guarding the precious water sources, so scant in the Holy Land, as well as Judaea's western approaches from the coastal plain. At 50 miles from Jerusalem, the commanding officer could feel secure enough to dispatch the main body of the guard—the infantry and the auxiliaries—back to Jerusalem, escorting Paul to Caesarea with seventy cavalrymen only.

A SLAVE BECOME KING

Caesarea, located halfway between Jaffa and Haifa, the ancient Straton's Tower, had been given by Augustus to Herod, who built it up splendidly and named it after his benefactor, Caesar Augustus. This is how Josephus describes it: "He rebuilt it all with white stone and adorned it with several most splendid palaces. He built a harbor larger than was the Piraeus at Athens and in the inner retirements of the water he built other deep stations for the ships also. There were also a great number of arches where the mariners dwelt. Now there were continual edifices joined to the harbor, which were also themselves of white stone; and to this harbor did the narrow streets of the city lead and were built at equal distances one from another. Upon an elevation there was a temple for Caesar which was excellent in beauty and largeness. He also built the amphitheater and theater and market place, and appointed games every fifth year and named them 'Caesar's Games'" (Wars 1:411). Water was brought by a large aqueduct from springs on the southern slope of the Carmel, eight miles away. All these edifices were erected in the astonishingly short time of 12

When they came to Caesarea, . . . they presented Paul also before him (Felix) *(Acts 23:33)*

Statues of Roman emperors found at Caesarea
made of red porphyry and white marble.
Since the heads of the statues were destroyed,
it is not possible to identify them.

years—small wonder, in a country where today cities are conjured up out of the desert, like Tel Aviv, which only seventy years ago was but a tiny village in the dunes of the Mediterranean.

In the year 6 AD Caesarea became the seat of the Roman procurators, and as such the capital of the Roman province of Judaea.

The population was predominantly heathen, but there was also a strong Jewish minority. Relations between the communities were strained, the tension erupting occasionally into violent conflicts. Both sides claimed ownership of the city: the Jews, because the city had been founded by a Jewish king, Herod; the heathen, because pagan temples were built under official auspices. It was in Caesarea that a bloody conflict precipitated the outbreak of the great revolt in 66 AD ending tragically in 70 with the sacking of Jerusalem and destruction of the Temple by Titus.

On arrival in Caesarea, Paul was brought before Felix who set a date for hearing the case when the accusing party was due to arrive. Five days later Paul's accusers arrived, Ananias among them. They brought several charges, either unsupported by evidence or irrelevant to Roman law—of agitation, attempt to profane the Temple and of being "a ringleader of the sect of the Nazarenes" (Acts 24:5). Asked by Felix to answer the charges, Paul countered that their accusations were unfounded and therefore could not be proved. He brilliantly refuted their charges, stressing that the only point of contention was in respect to the resurrection of the dead in which he believed implicitly. He reiterated that he was an observant Jew; "I worship the God of our fathers, believing everything laid down by the law or written in the prophets" (Acts 24:14). He had returned after several years to worship in Jerusalem, bringing alms and offerings to his people. "As I was doing this, they found me purified in the temple, without any crowd or tumult" (Acts 24:18). He was accused by some Jews from Asia, and they ought to be here before Felix to state what they had against him. Then he challenged his accusers to "say what wrongdoing they found when I stood before the council" except his assertion in the belief of the resurrection of the dead.

Felix was rather impressed by Paul's clear and precise reply, but since according to Roman law it was impossible to force a settlement of a complaint unsupported by evidence, he decided to stall. "When Lysias the tribune comes down, I will decide your case" (Acts 24:22), but in effect he put the matter off indefinitely.

Some days later, Felix and his Jewish wife Drusilla sent for Paul, wishing to hear him again. Felix was interested in hearing Paul on the philosophical aspect of his faith, but was not prepared to face his own conscience when "justice, self-control and future judgment" was mentioned, and dismissed him. However, he saw Paul often and enjoyed his conversations with him.

Felix' intellectual interests did in no way diminish his inane greed and corruption; he hoped the Christian community would come forth with a considerable bribe to have Paul freed. The brethren might have been willing to come along to secure Paul's release, but for Paul it would have been totally unacceptable, on religious as well as ethical grounds: "The donor of bribes is blamed as a temptor or accomplice of the taker."

The promulgation of the best laws does not yet assure justice to the individual. Much depends on those administering them. Thus Felix did not scruple to keep under arrest for two years a man whom he knew under the Roman law to be innocent. True, Paul's captivity was light, and restricted only his freedom of movement; he was allowed to receive as many visitors as he pleased and could, of course, keep servants to cater to his needs. These two years of enforced inactivity were not lost for Paul. He kept up and established closer contacts with Christians from Samaria and Galilee, as well as with those from Caesarea.

"TO CAESAR YOU SHALL GO"

Two years later (60 AD) Felix was replaced by Porcius Festus, who seemed to be a man of integrity. He immediately took up the case his predecessor had left unresolved and had a new examination of the case begun. Since he wanted to give his decision only after a further session in Jerusalem, Paul, who knew well what to expect there, regarded it as still another subterfuge. Refusing to be sacrificed for the sake of political convenience, he declared: "I am standing before Caesar's tribunal, where I ought to be tried; I appeal to Caesar.'" After a short consultation with his advisers, Festus conceded that Paul was within his rights: "You have appealed to Caesar; to Caesar you shall go" (Acts 25:10–12).

Some days later, Agrippa II accompanied by his sister Berenice came down to Caesarea from his northern kingdom to greet the new procurator. Agrippa's seat was at the sources of the Jordan river in Caesarea Philippi—founded by Philip, Herod's son. After Herod's death his kingdom had been divided into three tetrarchies, the northern falling under Philip's rule. Festus was glad to have Agrippa around at that moment, since he could not make out what Paul was actually accused of. For him it was only "certain points of dispute . . . about their own superstitions and about one Jesus, who was dead, but whom Paul asserted to be alive" (Acts 25:19). Since Festus was sending Paul to Caesar, it was essential to state a case, but the bewildered Roman, by his own assertion, had "nothing definite to write to my lord about him" (Acts 25:26). Agrippa's arrival was a boon from heaven; he would lend his prestige as a Jewish king and, though completely Hellenized, the authority of one well-versed in Jewish law. Thus Festus asked the king if he

would look into this case. When Agrippa asked to hear Paul himself, Festus agreed with alacrity. The following morning the meeting convened with "great pomp" in the "audience hall". Paul was brought in and Agrippa bade him make his defense. "Then Paul stretched out his hand . . ." in his characteristic gesture, and recounted his life—the mission he had received and his ministry, his beliefs, including the controversial one in resurrection, declaring himself fortunate to be able to make his defense before Agrippa who was "especially familiar with all customs and controversies of the Jews" (Acts 26:3), hoping he might find understanding of his case. He commanded the absolute attention of his listeners when he spoke of his faith, but when he stated his belief in resurrection, it was too much for Festus. The cultivated Roman, who could appreciate and subsequently gave tribute to Paul's great erudition and intellect, was unable to understand his preoccupation with such irrelevancies as resurrection and burst out: "Paul, you are mad; your great learning is turning you mad" (Acts 26:24). Paul countered that he was nothing of the kind, and taking the king as a witness, declared that he was

Concerts and other artistic performances take place today in the ancient amphitheater of Caesarea (below). The harbor of Caesarea (right) was thus described by the contemporary historian Josephus Flavius: "He (Herod) built a harbor larger than was the Piraeus of Athens."

'You have appealed to Caesar; to Caesar you shall go' (Acts 25:12)

Nero, the caesar to whom Paul appealed when Festus, the procurator of Judaea, found himself unable to resolve his case. Nero was notorious for his cruelty and corruption, and it was in his time that some of the most severe persecutions of the early Christians took place.

"speaking the sober truth." With the intensity so characteristic of him he appealed dramatically: "King Agrippa, do you believe the prophets? I know that you believe." But Agrippa got off with a light ironical remark: "In a short time you think to make me a Christian!" Paul's answer was dramatic and bold at the same time: "Whether short or long, I would to God that not only you but also all who hear me this day might become such as I am—except for these chains" (Acts 26:27–29).

Thus ended the hearing. The procurator, the king, Berenice and the suite left the hall. Privately they were of one opinion: the man had done nothing to deserve either death or imprisonment. Agrippa remarked to Festus, that, actually, had Paul not appealed to Caesar, he could have been set free, which implied, that since Paul had done so, Festus was well rid of him and the necessity of pronouncing judgment. Paul would go to Rome, to state his case before Caesar—the mad Nero.

O wild West Wind . . .
Thou who didst waken from his summer dreams
The blue Mediterranean . . .
(Percy Bysshe Shelley)

7. ROME, THE ETERNAL CITY

Why did Paul undertake it? The fact that he was a prisoner going to Rome under guard was immaterial, since had Paul been willing to compromise, he would not have had to go at all. Therefore the ultimate reason must be seen as Paul's unshakeable determination to reach the world's capital in whatever form, whether as a free man or a prisoner. He had clearly stated it as his aim in Ephesus when about to embark on his last journey to Jerusalem: "After I have been there, I must also see Rome" (Acts 19:21). Having preached the Gospel in Jerusalem, Samaria, Asia Minor and Greece, he felt that now he must go to Rome—the greatest Gentile city and the symbol of the Gentile world. But it was not his intention to see it as the end of the road. On the contrary, his dynamic personality could conceive nothing of the sort; he would "continue on the pilgrim way" (Davies) and return time and again to his homeland, Jerusalem.

THE MARINERS
Luke's account of Paul's journey to Rome is a marvel of graphic description, and one of the classical accounts in seafaring literature.

Since Judaea was not among the provinces sending regular supplies to Rome, ships calling at Caesarea bound for Rome must have been rare, especially so close to the season when shipping stopped altogether, owing to the approach of winter. Therefore, the best that could be found was a Greek vessel "from Adramyttium which was about to sail to the ports along the coast of Asia" (Acts 27:2). So Paul and several other prisoners were handed over "to a centurion of the Augustan Cohort named Julius" (Acts 27:1). The season was well advanced, "because the fast had already gone by." The fast referred to was obviously Yom Kippur, the Day of Atonement. A popular Jewish proverb ran: "When you bind your 'lulav', bind your ship." The "lulav," a palm frond, is used during the celebration of Succoth, the Festival of Booths, which follows Yom Kippur by three days. It is the time when the storms of the equinox begin, high and low pressure centers move in rapid sequence from west to east and then remain for a while over Cyprus, the so-called Cyprus low. The sharper the pressure gradients, the more violent the winds.

Since the winds did not permit a direct north-

191

There the centurion found a ship of Alexandria sailing for Italy and put us aboard (Acts 27:6)

Model of a Roman grain vessel (below) of the 2nd century A.D. reconstructed from a relief found in the port of Ostia. Bound for Italy, Paul's ship was sailing westward along the southern coast of Crete (right), when the dreaded northeaster struck them.

. . . we sailed under the lee of Crete . . . (Acts 27:7)

. . . we then learned that the island was called Malta (Acts 28:1)

Paul had gathered a bundle of sticks and put them on the fire when a viper came out . . . and fastened on his hand (Acts 28:3)

The fishing harbor of Malta. The Maltese, simple and compassionate folk received hospitably the shipwrecked party and extended them every assistance during their stay on the island. After reaching safely dry land, Paul and his companions set out to gather sticks to kindle a fire. When Paul deposited his bundle on the fire a viper (right) crept out and fastened onto his hand, but miraculously Paul was unharmed.

west course, Paul's ship, setting out from Caesarea, sailed north along the coast, and the following day put in at Sidon, the twin city of Tyre in Phoenicia. Julius, the centurion, was well inclined toward Paul and allowed him to go ashore to greet his friends. Thence the ship continued north, keeping east of Cyprus, in order to have some protection from the westerly wind. Obviously such vessels could not sail into the wind, so Paul's ship slowly made her way along the southern coast of Asia Minor to Myra in Lycia. Myra, a center of the grain trade, was known as a haven of refuge from the prevailing west winds. All that is left of Myra's former opulence is the ruins of a great amphitheater. Its other claim to fame was the 4th century bishop, St. Nicholas, the beloved saint of children, the Santa Claus of Christmas time.

THE WEST WIND

At Myra, the centurion found an Alexandrian merchantman engaged in the all important grain trade. The ship was on its way from Alexandria, the great harbor of Egypt, to Italy. This was one of the principal routes of the Mediterranean in Paul's time;

...on the second day we came to Puteoli (Acts 28:13)

Pozzuoli, ancient Puteoli in the Bay of Naples, where Paul landed to proceed on foot to Rome. Little is left of this magnificent harbor of Rome, since due to seismic movement most of the Roman city is submerged in the bay.

for the populace of Rome depended for their free distribution of wheat on the two great granaries of the Empire, Africa and Egypt. No wonder, therefore, that in spite of the late season the grain ships were still plying the Mediterranean. But unwilling to risk the open sea, the captain had preferred to sail along the coast and took his ship to Myra where her new passengers awaited her. Since the smaller vessel Paul and his companions arrived on was wintering in Myra, the centurion transferred his charges onto the Alexandrian grain-ship. In contrast to the naval vessels, such merchant ships used only sail-power; they were massively built with a big storage capacity. The frail craft of antiquity, square-rigged and with shallow draft, were an easy prey to the storms that swept the Mediterranean at that time of the year. If we consider that the largest ship of which we know in ancient times, an Alexandrian wheat ship of about 1,500 tons (as compared to the 30–40,000-ton vessels of today), was driven into port by rough weather and that a boat of 30 tons was already called a "ship" in the Mishna, we can understand why the ancient vessels hugged the coastline and did not venture upon the open seas at all in

And the brethren there, when they heard of us, came as far as the forum of Appius . . . to meet us *(Acts 28:15)*

Via Appia (left), the "queen of Roman roads". Paul too walked along this great ancient thoroughfare on his way to Rome. Funerary monuments (right) line both sides of the Appian way which also served the Romans as a cemetery.

winter. Paul's ship must have been fairly large and of the better class; estimated at 1,200 tons, it carried passengers and a crew as well as a cargo. The passengers were accommodated, as far as possible, in a cabin on the aft-deck or forecastle, men and women separated by a curtain. The grain was either poured into a storage room covered with boards on top, or was kept in sacks. The ship traveled at an average speed of 5 knots with a sail about 20 meters wide, made of white or multi-colored linen. There was also an auxiliary sail, which gave the ship its manoeverability. There were generally several anchors of about 25 kilograms each, as a rule four, which were fastened two by two to ropes. Only in cases of necessity was the plumb line, the so-called "holy anchor", used near coasts to sound the depth. During storms, the steering wheel was tied up. In order to strengthen the ship, chains or ropes were passed under the hull, either from fore to aft or from side to side. A small boat was taken along as rescue equipment.

Grain ships belonged to private companies; Alexandria, especially had its own association of shipowners. Paul's ship might have belonged to a Jewish

And so we came to Rome

(Acts 28:14)

Rome, the Eternal City at dusk.
View toward St. Peter's Square.

shipowner, which gives us an intimation of Paul's license to speak up freely with advice to the captain in the course of the journey. The captain had to tend to everything; he had often to climb to the top of the mast and sit there long hours scanning the vast horizon. The ship was manned by a motley crew of sailors, few of whom had sailing experience. They were rough-mannered, unreliable fellows who yet despised their passengers. Religiosity and superstition produced a strange mixture on board those vessels. Representation of such ships were found in certain holy places, in Jerusalem in the tomb of Jason, as well as near the pool of Bethesda.

The ship was already laden with grain when Paul and his companions embarked. Sailing slowly against the wind, the ship worked its way northward until it was just south of Cnidus, opposite Cos, "and as the wind did not allow us to go on" (Acts 27:7) she struck south to come under the lee of Crete (that is to the south of the island), passing by the promontory of Salmone. Under the protection of Crete, the ship with difficulty reached Fair Havens, near Lasea. Though a safe enough anchorage, Fair Havens was unsuitable for a prolonged stay and too

200

open to storms. But winter was already at hand and the problem was to find the best place to stay during the stormy months. Paul with his vast experience of sea travel advised wintering at Fair Havens in spite of its obvious drawbacks, "but the centurion paid more attention to the captain and to the owner of the ship than to what Paul said (Acts 27:11). Thus the sailors, will full knowledge of the risk, decided to try sailing west to Phoenix, a safe harbor.

Deceptively, a gentle south wind seemed to bear out that decision, so "they weighed anchor and sailed along Crete, close inshore" (Acts 27:13). And then disaster struck. The northeaster called Euroclydon (a composite Greek name, made up of the name for the northeast wind Euros, and klydon, "wave") caught them amidships and drove the vessel away from land. It came under the shelter of the small island of Cauda, and the crew sought to strengthen the ship for the strain of the storm, "to undergird" it, i.e. pass cables, either chains or ropes under the keel to prevent the timber from being tossed apart. They hoisted up the rescue boat—no easy feat in such seas. Then, for fear that the ship

Passing through the Roman Forum Paul could not fail to notice the great temple of Castor and Pollux dedicated to the Dioscuri, the famous Twin Brothers, protectors of mariners, under whose sign he sailed from Malta to Italy. The three slender columns (foreground right) are today the only vestige of the temple. Seen in the background is Titus' Arch, erected to commemorate his capture of Jerusalem in 70 A.D.

. . . we set sail in a ship of Alexandria, with the Twin Brothers as a figurehead (Acts 28:11)

Begun by the emperor Flavius Vespasian
and completed by his son Titus in 80 A.D.,
the elliptical mass of the Colosseum remains
an enduring symbol of Rome.
The Amphitheatrum Flavium has been known
as the Colosseum since the Middle Ages due
to its colossal dimensions—capable of
holding 50,000 spectators. The largest in
antiquity, it was the arena of the bloodiest
gladiatorial fights.

might be driven into Syrtis Major (the gulf of the treacherous shallows off the northern coast of Africa between Tripolitania and Cyrenaica), they lowered the sail and so were driven by the gale. To lighten the ship, they began by throwing the cargo overboard, and finally cast out the tackle of the ship too. For days they drifted, not having the least idea where they were. This is quite understandable, if we remember that navigation was entirely by the stars and the sun, without any of the appliances which were known even in the Middle Ages, such as the compass. This meant that there was no possibility of ascertaining the position of the ship on cloudy nights. So, "when neither sun nor stars appeared for many a day, and no small tempest lay on us, all hope of our being saved was at last abandoned" (Acts 27:20). When despair gripped all present on board, Paul took charge. He could not refrain from reminding them that should they have listened to his advice—the pleasure of pronouncing the words "I told you so" is one of the irresistible foibles of man—they would not have found themselves in those straits. But now he bid them "take heart, for there will be no loss of life among you, but only of the ship. An angel of the God to whom I belong and whom I worship . . ." (Acts 27:21–24) announced this to him that very night in an epiphany so typical of sea-farers.

THE ROAR OF SURF ON THE ROCKS

Unknowingly, they were driven by the gale westward, "across the sea of Adria", a name which in antiquity was applied also to the open sea west of Crete. After fourteen days of wild buffeting, the ship appeared to be drawing near the land during the night. The crew probably heard the roaring surf on the rocks above the howl of the tempest, and they immediately took soundings with the plumb line. The first cast showed a depth of twenty fathoms. The next sounding was only 15 fathoms. As the water became steadily more shallow, the danger now arose of the boat being dashed to pieces on the rocks. The sailors then cast four anchors from the stern, hoping to ride out the storm, at least till daylight. Some of the sailors, though, desperate after a fortnight of torment—seasickness, hunger, and uncertainty—realizing that land was near, tried to reach it by abandoning ship in the rescue boat. Paul

The remains of the great synagogue at Ostia, the port of Rome at the mouth of the Tiber. This is the only synagogue of this period thus far found in western Europe.

MAMERTINUM

LA PRIGIONE DEI SS. APOSTOLI

PIETRO E PAOLO

IL PIÙ ANTICO CARCERE DI ROMA

XXV SECOLI DI STORIA

The notorious Mamertine prison where, according to tradition, Peter and Paul were imprisoned during the Neronian persecutions of Christians following the great fire in Rome in the year 64 A.D.

saw what was happening and at once told the centurion. "The soldiers then cut away the ropes of the boat and let it go."

At dawn, Paul's composure and control of the situation became evident. If the ship were to break up, the passengers and crew would have to swim to land, a strenuous physical exertion in such seas at any time, and more so for people laid low by prolonged seasickness. He understood that they would have to build up stamina for what lay ahead. Out of superstitious belief the crew and the passengers used to fast when the ship was in danger of wreckage: "Today is the fourteenth day that you have continued in suspense and without food, having taken nothing." But the sages sternly opposed it, fearing that the sailors' physical condition and their ability to work would be impaired. Therefore he continued: "I urge you to take some food; it will give you strength..." (Acts 27:34). To this he added the reassurance that all would be saved. Setting a personal example, this extraordinary man, in the wildly tossed ship and in the face of imminent shipwreck, calmly "took bread and giving thanks to God in the presence of all he broke it and began to eat" (Acts 27:35). His supreme composure and unshakeable faith cheered the company. They ate their fill, and threw the remaining wheat overboard to lighten the ship still more.

When day broke, they found themselves in a bay, but neither the captain nor anybody else recognized it. However, the one chance of safety lay in beaching the ship—if only they could get to the beach! Weighing the anchors and lowering the rudders into the sea, they hoisted the foresail and made for land. But the gale still blew fiercely, and caught between wildly dashing currents, the ship struck a shoal. "The bow stuck and remained unmovable, and the stern was broken by the surf" (Acts 27:41). The soldiers wanted to kill the prisoners lest they escape, but the centurion, wishing to save Paul, ordered all who could swim to throw themselves into the sea, while the others clung to the wreckage and were washed ashore by the waves. Paul's words came true—all were saved. It turned out that they had landed at a bay on the island of Malta—the scene of the most famous shipwreck in history.

SHIPWRECKED ON MALTA

The traditional place where they came ashore was the so-called St. Paul's creek. Malta is the largest of five islands at the eastern end of the straits between Sicily and Tunis. It has been inhabited since prehistoric times, but the settlers of whom we have historical knowledge were the Phoenicians of Carthage. Their Semitic language, a dialect of Phoenician, is still spoken on the island, which became part of the Roman empire after the Punic wars and the fall of Carthage.

The inhabitants were highly skilled artisans and artists as well as prosperous traders. They produced valuable textiles, especially linen. The Phoenicians were always famous for their artistic weaving—especially valued were their fine purple fabrics. Blessed with good harbors, the Maltese traded in the best tradition of the enterprising Phoenicians.

The shipwrecked party were kindly received by the natives, compassionate folk, who welcomed them, and since "it had begun to rain and was cold" (Acts 28:2) started to kindle a fire to warm the wet and shivering strangers. They all set about gathering fuel for the fire, when a strange incident

Named after the apostle the Porta S. Paolo is the old Porta Ostiensis through which, according to tradition, Paul was led out of the city on his last journey—to the place of his execution. The road leading to Ostia, Rome's harbor, passed through this gate, hence its name in antiquity.

occurred, repeated by superstitious seafarers all over the world, when sitting together in the evenings and listening to storytellers' tales of wonder: "Paul had gathered a bundle of sticks and put them on the fire, when a viper came out because of the heat and fastened on his hand" (Acts 28:3). The bystanders, especially the natives, when they "saw the creature hanging from his (Paul's) hand" were understandably shocked: "No doubt this man is a murderer." How else could it be understood, but that "though he has escaped from the sea, justice has not allowed him to live" (Acts 28:4). Paul merely "shook off the creature into the fire and suffered no harm." But the natives were not convinced. He might yet "swell up or suddenly fall down dead." So they "waited a long time and saw no misfortune come to him."

This unusual incident prompted the conclusion that this uncanny stranger, far from being a murderer, was actually a god!

Under the main church of Rabat, a grotto is pointed out in which Paul is supposed to have lived while on Malta. Many visitors carry away with them little stones as protection against snake-bite;

the little stones allegedly crop up again at night. Legends of snakes and precious stones were also told by Jewish seafarers, and certainly go back to old Phoenician traditions.

As their wreck had occurred in the neighborhood of the estate of Publius, "the chief man of the island", Paul and his companions were soon introduced to him. He received them kindly and entertained them hospitably for three days.

Since it was now clear that they would have to winter on the island, which meant at least three months' stay, they could not impose upon their hosts for so long. It would also have been much against Paul's long established principle that a man should earn his living. They therefore moved to their own quarters. When Publius' father fell ill "with fever and dysentery" Paul visited him and cured the old man. This of course put them in very high esteem with the populace and attracted all the other ailing people on the island. The Maltese gave generous expression to their gratitude, so that by the time Paul's group left the island, they were richly equipped with whatever they might need.

WESTWARD UNDER THE SIGN OF "THE TWINS"

Three months later they boarded another wheat ship, also from Alexandria, which had been luckier than their own vessel and was wintering on Malta, bound for Italy.

Like most vessels of ancient times, this one too was dedicated to some god, in this case to Castor and Pollux, the Dioscuri, the twin children of Zeus by Leda. The two youths, whose emblem was a high cap with a star above it, were the protectors of mariners. No doubt the images of the twins were engraved on the ship's poop, as was usual with ancient ships.

They crossed safely to Syracuse, an excellent harbor, where they stayed for three days. Numerous catacombs and ancient churches show that the Way took hold early in that once famous city. A unique feature, its cathedral, once a temple to Pallas Athena, is now the only Doric temple which is still a religious sanctuary.

From Syracuse, sailing due north, they passed through the Straits of Messina, the location of the dreaded mythical Scylla and Charibdis, and on to Rhegium, at the very tip of the Italian boot. They then continued northwards, sailing along that beautiful Italian coast, up to the Gulf of Naples, past Tiberius' palace on Capri, past doomed Pompeii and Herculaneum. The sumptuous villas of the rich lay in the ominous shade of the deceptive serenity of Vesuvius, which 19 years later was to cover with horror and ashes the magnificent, depraved cities of the smiling bay. Finally they came to Puteoli, the harbor of Rome, north of modern Naples.

Puteoli with its Solfatara—the crater of a semi-extinguished volcano—its hot springs and gracious temple of Serapis, its sweeping view over the Gulf, was indeed a marvelous city. Since it was a favored port for large ships coming from Egypt, it must have been a thriving, mighty and—judging by the frescoes of Pompeii—bawdy harbor. Much of it is now under water, due to seismic movement. The atmosphere in such a port town is little conducive to spiritual preoccupations; yet surprisingly, in this most unlikely milieu, Paul and his companions found Christian "brethren and were invited to stay with them for seven days" (Acts 28:14).

From Puteoli the party traveled on foot to Rome

'O death, where is thy victory?' *(I Corinthians 15:55)*

along the famous Via Appia, the "Queen of the Roman Roads". The villas and monumental tombs lining the Appian Way make an unforgettable impression as one draws nearer to the great capital. Acts has nothing to say about any of these beautiful sights which gladden the heart of every traveler. But it reflects the mentality of Paul, who had eyes only for human beings. According to the Oriental custom and as a sign of hospitality, Christians from Rome came out halfway to greet Paul: the first met him at the beginning of the Pontine Marshes some forty miles from Rome, at Forum Apii, a hamlet which according to the poet Horace was an "Eldorado for seamen, pub-keepers and other shady characters."

More Christian brethren were waiting for him at "Tres Tabernae", the Three Taverns, some 33 miles from the capital. Paul was deeply touched. "On seeing them Paul thanked God and took courage" (Acts 28:15). Finally the party reached the Alban hills—and there, below, lay Rome.

Upon arrival in Rome, the centurion turned Paul over to the prefect of the imperial praetorian guard. His case was further complicated by the loss of all

An oasis of peace, the Trappist monastery of Tre Fontane (Three Springs) dating from the 7th century. Here, in a small pine grove by the Sylvian Marsh about three miles from Rome, Paul was beheaded. The chapel preserves the memory of the apostle.

the pertinent documents in the shipwreck. Therefore he was not imprisoned but allowed instead to live in his own quarters, rented at his own expense, his freedom limited only by the custody of a Roman guard.

THE GRANDEUR THAT WAS ROME

What was the Rome Paul had come to? A modern visitor, musing over the monuments and remnants of the ancient city, is awed by its grandeur. Yet most of the magnificent edifices were not yet there in Paul's time, not the three triumphal arches of Titus, Septimus Severus and Constantine, nor the Colosseum, nor the columns of Trajan and Marcus Aurelius.

When at certain intervals Paul had to report to the imperial tribunal on the Palatine, his way lead through the Forum Romanum with its temples to Vesta, Castor and Pollux as well as the two basilicas, Emilian and Julian. He saw the forum of Augustus and on top of the Capitol the temple of Jupiter, Juno and Minerva. The Mausoleum of Augustus and the magnificent "Ara Pacis" (the Altar of Peace) brought memories of the emperor's testa-

ment which he had read in Pisidian Antioch. It is characteristic of Paul that he has nothing to say of the beauty of the city on the seven hills, its splendid market-places, its temples and stadiums. Here too, only the idea of spreading his faith moved him.

Rome was a city of great social differences: we are struck with wonder at the sight of the villas of the great patricians, as exemplified by the house of Livia, Augustus' empress, with its fabulous mosaics. All the more dismaying is the sight of the several-storied, barrack-like buildings—the rented dwellings of the poor—whose architectural exterior with its numerous windows was in marked contrast to the miserable, unhygienic condition of the interior. And there were the idle crowds of dispossessed masses awaiting either the dole to which they had grown accustomed, or entertainment. There were also the Oriental Syrian upstarts and snobs living at the court of Nero, described by Petronius in his "Banquet of Trimalchio". In Roman night-life Syrian boys and girls were in great demand.

"THAT THEY SHOULD SEEK GOD"

The old state religions, as illustrated on the Ara

Pacis, with their sacrifices and processions, could not satisfy the people's spiritual yearnings. This satisfaction they looked for and found in the mystery cults of the Orient. As early as 205 BC the black stone, representing the great mother Cybele, an ancient Oriental worship symbol, had been introduced to Rome. Others followed, such as Isis from Egypt, Astarte from Syria, and Mithras, the sun-god whose fight against darkness was represented in the mystery-grottoes, which may have been known to Paul, since one of them has recently been excavated in Israel at Caesarea.

All sorts of itinerant priests of various eastern deities went about proclaiming, to the raucous accompaniment of brass and cymbals, the qualities of the gods they served.

Such was the Rome that Paul encountered. This was the capital of the empire that held the world in its hands. And if in Paul's view he was the messenger of the world's salvation, then his arrival in Rome was both timely and indispensable, for he could only fulfill his mission by operating in and from that world's center.

The Jewish community in the 1st century BC may be considered of special importance. It was concentrated on the right bank of the Tiber (the Travestere), where the ancient ghetto still stands. The Ponte Rotto dates from Paul's time. The Jews were occasionally involved in political and social dissensions and sided with the "populares" against the ruling aristocracy. They were conspicuous in the mourning of Julius Caesar (44 BC). Their status deteriorated under the emperors Tiberius and Caligula: many were exiled, but these measures were not of long duration. The majority were "little people": shopkeepers, tailors, tentmakers, as well as beggars and peddlers, at whose raucous activities the Roman satirists poked fun. Of the thirteen synagogues mentioned in literature nothing is preserved. But at Ostia, a great synagogue was excavated in 1961, which is the only one of the period thus far found in Western Europe. Especially noteworthy are its marble columns and mosaic floors, the Jewish symbols carved in the tabernacle, a special room for baking "matzot", a ritual bath, and a classroom. In Rome there are also six Jewish burial catacombs, whose 500 inscriptions give an idea of the life of the community.

The statue of Paul graces the entrance to the Basilica of S. Paolo fuori le Mura (St. Paul Outside the Walls). Here, over the lonely grave of the apostle on the way to Ostia, Constantine the Great founded the Basilica of Paul. The Byzantine style fresco above the apse (right) represents Christ flanked by the apostles Luke, Paul Peter and Andrew.

Three days after his arrival Paul called together the leaders of the very sizeable Jewish community, estimated at that time at 30,000 people. Presuming they knew all about him, he told them that contrary to what they had heard, he had done nothing to harm the Jewish people, its traditions and teaching. He said he had been falsely accused and delivered to the Romans, who had found no guilt with him under their laws, and would have let him go free, but because of the accusations leveled against him in Jerusalem he had been "compelled to appeal to Caesar." He said he felt an inner need to tell his own people that, not only had he done nothing inimical to them, but rather "because of the hope of Israel that I am bound with this chain" (Acts 28:20). The Jewish elders replied tactfully that they had heard nothing from Judaea about Paul, and would be interested to hear him on the subject, since they had to admit they knew that the new faith "is everywhere spoken against." They set a date for the assembly and came "at his lodging in great numbers." Paul expounded his creed of God basing his arguments on Moses and the Prophets. "Some were convinced by what he said, while others disbelieved"

(Acts 28:24). Before they departed, Paul warned them, that if they were deaf to his teaching, the salvation of God would be sent to the Gentiles: they would listen.

Paul settled down in Rome "and lived there two whole years at his own expense and welcomed all who came to him, preaching the kingdom of God and teaching about the Lord Jesus Christ quite openly and unhindered" (Acts 28:30). Thus ends the book of Acts. By making Rome his center Paul had achieved his goal. At this moment, Paul, the man, recedes into the background. A veil envelops him, warning us not to approach too near his mystery.

EPILOGUE

Paul's last days are shrouded in mystery. That he intended to visit Spain we know, but not if he ever went there. Whatever came down to us of his life after the year 62—that he was acquitted and released and traveled to Spain (where the church of Tarragona preserves his memory), then returned to Rome, was tried again, jailed, perhaps in the notorious Carcer Mamertinum underneath the Capitol, condemned to death and that he subsequently died a

martyr's death during the Neronian persecutions of Christians following the great fire of 64—comes from much later sources (end of 2nd century), namely the apocryphal "Acts of Paul". These are mainly legendary and no reliable evidence. We do not even know the year of his death. On the other hand, the place of his execution is pointed out by an early and constant tradition. He was led out of the city through the Porta Ostiensis, to a small pine grove where today we find the Trappist monastery of Tre Fontane. It is an old monastery in Rome, originally a church established in the 7th century. According to tradition supported by the evidence of Tacitus that execution outside the walls was indeed a Roman custom, this is the site of Paul's death. Here he was beheaded.

According to a legend, the head of the apostle was struck down three times upon the ground. In these places three springs have miraculously burst forth, and over them was built the church of Tre Fontane, now an oasis of peace.

He was buried in a grave on the road to Ostia, over which the great Basilica of Paul was to rise. During the persecutions under Valerian in the year

258, his remains, like those of Peter, were transferred to the catacombs of St. Sebastian on the Appian Way, where they were apparently put for safekeeping in an unknown grave. Graffiti with the name of the apostle and the mention of a wake indicate the reverence of Paul's small community for his earthly remains. Some 40 years later, the remains of Paul were replaced in their original burial site, over which a modest church was built by Constantine in the 4th century. Constantine's old basilica over the apostle's grave was successively enlarged through the centuries and enriched with frescoes and mosaics. Magnificent cloisters were added in the thirteenth century. These still remain, but the basilica was completely destroyed by fire in 1823. Of the original structure, only the apse mosaic and some restored mosaic fragments remain; and of the accumulated work of fourteen centuries only the columns and the external walls still stand. The church was restored in 1854 and on the site of the Byzantine church rose the magnificent Basilica of S. Paolo fuori le Mura, St. Paul's outside the Walls.

Saul, the Jew from Tarsus, rests in eternal Rome under the canopy of one of the most beautiful churches in the world, shadowed by a forest of pillars which appears to stretch into infinity. In this shrine ended Paul's earthly travels.

Here he can rest from his labors and sufferings, after having borne the mission of his Lord, in a triumphal procession, to the heart of the then known world. But one question remains: what was his stand toward his people whom he loved so warmly and by whom he so often felt himself misunderstood? We open the letter to the Romans and find the answer: "As regards election they are beloved for the sake of their forefathers; for the gifts and the call of God are irrevocable" (Rom. 11:28). We see before us an olive tree whose branches were cut off and wild descendants have sprouted up; but even these draw their sap from the old root.

A man of whom could be said:

"Thou, whose exterior semblance doth belie
  Thy soul's immensity;
Thou best philosopher, who yet dost keep
Thy heritage, thou eye among the blind,
That, deaf and silent, read'st the eternal deep,
Haunted forever by the eternal mind—..."

(W. Wordsworth)

221

The interior of the Basilica of St. Paul Outside the Walls—one of the most beautiful churches in the world. Under its lofty roof, overshadowed by a forest of pillars, rests Paul at the end of his earthly travels.

Paul, a servant of Jesus Christ, called to be an apostle, . . .

(Romans 1:1)

. . . thou hast crowned him with glory and honour, . . .

(Hebrews 2:7)

223

Baeck, Lee *Paulus, die Phärisaer und das Neue Testament.* Frankfurt 1961.

Ben Chorin, Shalom *Paulus. Der Völkerapostel in jüdischer Sicht.* München 1970.

Blank, Josef *Paulus und Jesus.* Múnchen 1968.

Bornkamm, Guenther *Paul.* New York 1971.

Davies, W. D. *Paul and Rabbinic Judaism.* London 1948.

Debelius, Martin *Paulus.* Berlin 1956.

Hengel, Martin *Judentum und Hellenismus.* Tübingen 1969.

Holzner, Joseph *Paul of Tarsus.* St. Louis 1944.

Lieberman, Saul *Hellenism in Jewish Palestine.* New York 1950.

Meinardus, Otto *St. Paul in Greece.* Athens 1973.

Meinardus, Otto *St. Paul in Ephesus and the cities of Galatia and Cyprus.* Athens 1975.

Michaelis, Wilhelm *Die apokryphen Schriften zum Neuen Testament.* Bremen 1958.

Morton, H. V. *In the Steps of St. Paul.* London 1936.

Perowne, Stewart *The Journeys of St. Paul.* London 1975.

Ramsay, William *The Cities of St. Paul.* London 1907

Ramsay, William *St. Paul the Traveller and the Roman Citizen.* London 1895.

Rigaux, Beda *St. Paul et ses lettres.* Paris 1964.

Safrai, S.–Stern, M. *The Jewish People in the First Century.* Assen 1974.

Schoeps, Hans-Joachim *Paul. The Theology of the Apostle in the Light of Jewish Religious History.* London 1961.

Schuerer, Emil *The History of the Jewish People in the Age of Jesus Christ.* A new English version. Edinburgh 1973.

Tcherikover, V. *Hellenistic Civilization and the Jews.* Philadelphia 1959.

Werfel, Franz *Paulus unter den Juden.* Wien 1926.